♔

CAKESMITHS
CAKES FOR COFFEE SHOPS

DEAR GREEN®

decent
PACKAGING

shibui leaf
tea

STORY
SHOP

US V THEM
ENGINEERING
COFFEE

FOR BREW FREAKS, BEAN GEEKS

AND THE SIMPLY CURIOUS ...

Independent Coffee Guide team:

Richard Bailey, Stephanie Boxall,
Nick Cooper, Charlotte Cummins,
Kathryn Lewis, Melissa Morris,
Christopher Mulholland, Tamsin Powell,
Jo Rees, Rosanna Rothery, Melissa Stewart,
Mark Tibbles and Selena Young.

A big thank you to the Independent Coffee
Guide committee (meet them on page 138)
for their expertise and enthusiasm, and our
partners Cakesmiths, Dear Green Coffee
Roasters, Decent Packaging, Shibui Tea,
Story Shop and Us V Them.

Coffee shops, cafes and roasteries are
invited to be included in the guide based
on meeting criteria set by the committee,
which includes the use of speciality beans,
providing a high-quality coffee experience
for visitors and being independently run.

For information on Independent Coffee
Guides for: England – The North, Midlands
and East; Southern England; Ireland;
and Wales, visit:

indycoffee.guide

⬡ *@indycoffeeguide*

© Salt Media Ltd

Published by Salt Media Ltd 2022

saltmedia.co.uk

01271 859299

ideas@saltmedia.co.uk

CONTENTS

WELCOME

One of my favourite things about the Scottish speciality scene is the diversity of its venues. From coffee bars jammed into former police boxes in Edinburgh to uber-modern cafes nestled in the wilds of the Highlands, each coffee shop, cafe and roastery offers a unique experience.

Like a coffee-loving friend with connections across the country, this book is designed to guide you to the best speciality spots in Scotland. You know the kind of places: those little backstreet brew bars hidden in plain sight, the off-the-beaten-track roastery cafes, and the multifaceted venues that also happen to craft a damn good flat white.

Whether you're planning a Glasgow city break or a roadtrip through the Scottish Borders, you'll find venues that surprise and excite. Happily, first-class speciality coffee is no longer solely the reserve of the cities and now some of the best beans in the country are roasted, brewed and served on small islands and in rural areas.

Feeling restless to hit the road on the trail of top-notch brews? There's never been a better time to pack a copy of the guide, a reusable cup and a sense of adventure and head out to explore Scotland's very special coffee scene.

Kathryn Lewis

Editor

Indy Coffee Guides

○ @indycoffeeguide

HOW TO USE THE GUIDE

CAFES

Find coffee shops and cafes where you can drink top-notch speciality coffee. We've split the guide into areas to help you discover places near you.

ROASTERIES

Meet the leading speciality coffee roasters in Scotland and discover where to source beans. Find them after the cafes in each area.

MAPS

Every cafe and roastery has a number so you can find them either on the area map at the start of each section or on the detailed city maps.

MORE GOOD STUFF

Discover **More good cups** and **More good roasteries** at the back of the book.

Follow us on social

@indycoffeeguide

YOUR
ADVENTURES
START
HERE

MAPS

We've split Scotland into areas to make it easier for you to find coffee shops and roasteries.

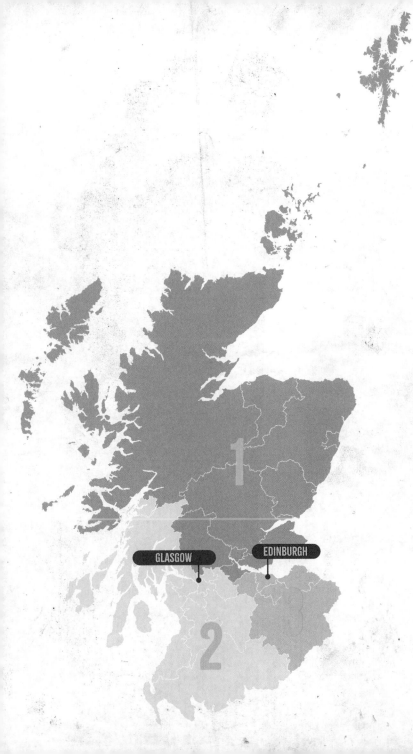

GLASGOW

EDINBURGH

1

2

3

AREA

1

● CAFES

1　Twenty One
2　Archive Coffee
3　Temple Harris
4　The Dunvegan
5　Caora Dhubh Coffee Company
6　Birch
7　Cafe Sia
8　Lean To Coffee
9　Slaughterhouse Coffee
10　Batchen Street Coffee
11　Speyside Coffee Roasting Co.
12　The Coffee Apothecary – Ellon
13　The Coffee Apothecary – Udny
14　Dreamy Goat Coffee Co.
15　Foodstory Uni
16　Foodstory Hut
17　Faffless
18　The Cult of Coffee
19　Foodstory
20　Figment
21　Ride Coffee House
22　Birdhouse Cafe
23　EH9 Espresso
24　Spoiled Life
25　The Roasting Project
26　HBW Coffee

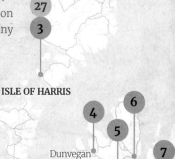

ISLE OF HARRIS

Dunvegan
Carbost
Portree
SKYE　Broad

● ROASTERIES

27　Temple Harris Coffee Roasters
28　Vandyke Brothers Coffee
29　Maison Dieu Coffee Roasters
30　Sacred Grounds Coffee Company
31　The Bean Shop
32　The Roasting Project
33　Stirling Coffee

Find more good cafes and roasteries on pages 132–137

All locations are approximate

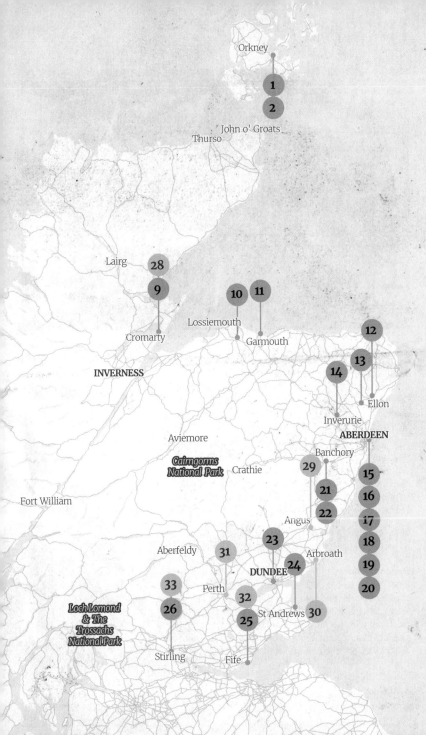

1 TWENTY ONE

21 Albert Street, Kirkwall, Orkney Islands, KW15 1HP

Reputation and diversification are essential when running a hospitality venue in Orkney; it's the only way to guarantee trade in the quiet months that bracket the high-season influx of tourists. Luckily, Twenty One has all bases covered: a bustling coffee shop and lunch stop by day, it becomes a cocktail bar and small-plates restaurant at night.

Coffee creds are high at the Albert Street venue, thanks to input from the team at sister business Archive Coffee. The satisfying house espresso comes courtesy of Glasgow's Dear Green but, if you're after something stronger, there's also an excellent selection of craft beers and cocktails available.

INSIDER'S TIP — SUCKER FOR SUCCULENT CHICKEN WINGS? DON'T MISS WING IT WEDNESDAY

The decor takes its cue from the modern American diner, with red banquette seating, glossy tiles and a black and white chequered floor. A wall of luscious leafy plants is an eye-catching focal point. For a cosy catch-up with friends, bag a booth and munch on globally inspired small plates such as the salt and chilli cauliflower po boy, and Korean broccoli.

ESTABLISHED
2019

KEY ROASTER
Dear Green
Coffee Roasters

BREWING METHOD
Espresso

MACHINE
La Marzocco
Linea PB

GRINDER
Mazzer Super
Jolly,
Mazzer Mini

OPENING HOURS
Mon-Tue
11am-5pm
Wed-Sat
11am-late

Gluten FREE

WIFI

DISABLED ACCESS

BRING YOUR OWN Cup.

01856 871228
f @twentyonekirkwall @twentyone_kirkwall

2 ARCHIVE COFFEE

The Old Library, 8 Laing Street, Kirkwall, Orkney Islands, KW15 1NW

There aren't many places in Orkney to drink on-point espresso so, if you're visiting the archipelago, a stop at Archive is a must.

Bang in the centre of Kirkwall, this popular cafe is housed in the town's former library. It has a high-beamed ceiling and spacious bar area where the day's line-up of tempting homemade cakes is paraded.

 TAKE A REUSABLE CUP AND GET 20P OFF COFFEE TO-GO

The house beans are supplied by Dear Green in Glasgow and bolstered by a roll call of guest coffees from other Scottish roasteries such as Sacred Grounds and Machina. If you taste something you like, you can recreate the magic at home by picking up a bag from the retail shelves.

Thanks to its relaxed community vibe and kid-friendly bakes, it's popular with families and quickly fills up during the day. For a quieter and more contemplative experience, get there early and supplement your morning coffee with brunch – stalwart dishes include pancakes topped with blueberries and lemon curd, and poached eggs with black pudding, hollandaise and crisp onions.

ESTABLISHED
2017

KEY ROASTER
Dear Green
Coffee Roasters

BREWING METHOD
Espresso

MACHINE
La Marzocco
Linea PB

GRINDER
Mazzer Kold,
Mazzer Mini,
Mazzer Super Jolly

OPENING HOURS
Mon–Sat
8.30am–5pm
Sun
11am–4pm

 Gluten FREE

 BEANS AVAILABLE INSTORE

 OUTDOOR seating

 DISABLED ACCESS

 BRING YOUR OWN Cup

01856 871228
 @archivecoffeekirkwall @archivecoffeekirkwall

3 TEMPLE HARRIS

22 Northton, Isle of Harris, HS3 3JA

Temple Coffee Roasters on the Isle of Harris is the UK's most westerly roastery and this sister cafe is where tourists and islanders go to sample its spoils.

All about provenance, the cafe was established in 2019 as a welcoming space where the Harris community could enjoy food made from locally grown ingredients and great coffee. Temple Harris is surrounded by spectacular scenery and its alfresco tables provide epic views across the water to the mountains. If it's blowing a hoolie, inside is a snug spot to hunker down.

TRY A STICKY MACHAIR BUN, THE TEAM'S OWN INVENTION MADE WITH WILD MEADOWSWEET

The team have always been keen to craft as much of their food and drink menu in-house as possible, which is what led to a roasting wing being added in 2022. The coffee line-up is roasted in a state-of-the-art Probat and headlined by the Temple Seasonal Espresso Blend.

This is supplemented by single origins from Guatemala, Brazil, Ethiopia, Peru, El Salvador and Colombia. Beans are sold on-site, along with deli goodies such as island sourdough and award-winning non-alcoholic spirit Wild Eve.

ESTABLISHED
2019

KEY ROASTER
Temple Coffee Roasters

BREWING METHOD
Espresso, filter, pourover, syphon

MACHINE
Conti CC202

GRINDER
Ceado E37J

OPENING HOURS
Wed–Sun
9.30am–4.30pm
(seasonal opening hours)

 Gluten FREE

 BEANS AVAILABLE INSTORE

 WIFI

 CYCLE FRIENDLY

 OUTDOOR seating

 BRING YOUR OWN Cup

 DOG FRIENDLY

templeharris.com   07979 926831
f @thetempleharris   @thetempleharris   @thetempleharris

4 THE DUNVEGAN

Main Street, Dunvegan, Isle of Skye, IV55 8WA

Thanks to its striking views over Loch Dunvegan, this restaurant, cafe and deli with rooms makes for a picturesque pit stop as you travel through the north west of Skye.

The cafe is open daily for speciality coffee from Dear Green plus a tempting assortment of homemade bakes. Such is The Dunvegan's rep for good bakes and brews that a steady stream of international visitors join the locals for a caffeine and cake fix with a side of epic loch views.

 INSIDER'S TIP **VISIT AT LUNCH TO CHOW DOWN THE LIKES OF HOMEMADE BURGERS, TACOS AND KEBABS**

While the coffee and cake combos are a draw, it's the wood-fired evening menu that has cemented The Dunvegan's status in Skye's food and drink scene. Taking inspiration from Argentina's asado culture, the talented chefs elevate Scottish produce using British charcoal and wood from FSC sources. They also love to cure, smoke and pickle seasonal ingredients – expect to tuck into dishes such as flame-licked Sconser scallops, Highland lamb and local lobster.

Sustainability is the watchword at The Dunvegan: food is sourced as locally as possible and the menus planned meticulously to minimise food waste.

ESTABLISHED
2019

KEY ROASTER
Dear Green
Coffee Roasters

BREWING METHOD
Espresso

MACHINE
La Marzocco

GRINDER
Compak

OPENING HOURS
Tue–Sat
11am–3.30pm
(dinner from 6pm)

 Gluten FREE

 BEANS AVAILABLE INSTORE

 WIFI

 OUTDOOR seating

 BRING YOUR OWN Cup

 DOG FRIENDLY

thedunvegan.com 01470 521497

f @thedunveganskye 🐦 @thedunveganskye ◎ @thedunveganskye

5 CAORA DHUBH COFFEE COMPANY

Carbost, Isle of Skye, IV47 8SR

C aora Dhubh (pronounced *Coo-ra Doo*) translates as "Black Sheep" in Gaelic – a fitting name for a venue that likes to do things a little differently.

Situated in a Scandi-style wooden building near the Talisker Whisky distillery on the banks of Loch Harport, this coffee shop is known as much for its fun-loving barista banter and quirky branding as for its first-rate coffee, toasted sandwiches and cakes.

 INSIDER'S TIP — CHECK OUT ARTWORK BY GLASGOW ARTIST JAMIE JOHNSON ON CAORA DHUBH'S COFFEE BAGS

The cafe opened in 2017 and in 2021 the team started roasting their own beans, so now a visit to this island coffee shop feels even more authentic. The team have also introduced some cutting-edge tech to this sleepy corner of Skye: a new Decent Espresso machine allows the baristas to customise every step of the espresso shot – from flow to temperature to weight – via tablet.

Alongside this pursuit of the perfect 'spro, owner Jamie Fletcher is committed to sustainability. Caora Dhubh is a takeaway-only joint, so customers are encouraged to bring their own cups, ready to be filled before venturing back outside to soak up the breathtaking Carbost scenery.

ESTABLISHED
2017

KEY ROASTER
Caora Dhubh
Coffee Company

BREWING METHOD
Espresso, filter,
Clever Dripper

MACHINE
La Marzocco
FB70, Decent
Espresso
DE1XXL

GRINDER
Mythos One x 2,
Mahlkonig EK43

OPENING HOURS
Mon–Sun
10am–5pm
(seasonal opening hours)

 Gluten FREE

 BEANS AVAILABLE INSTORE

 WIFI

 CYCLE FRIENDLY

 OUTDOOR seating

 DISABLED ACCESS

 BRING YOUR OWN Cup

 DOG FRIENDLY

caoradhubh.com **07827 012468**
f @caoradhubhcoffee @caoracoffee

6 BIRCH

Bayfield Road, Portree, Isle of Skye, IV51 9EL

A stark contrast to its rugged setting on the Isle of Skye, Birch is all clean lines, natural colour palette and curated ceramics. It's a beautiful slice of design-led minimalism and the perfect spot to find sanctuary from the island's often wild weather.

The influence of Melbourne's renowned speciality scene on founder Niall Munro is discernible in both the interiors and the emphasis on quality coffee and food. Shortly after opening Birch in July 2020, Niall started roasting coffee and now stocks the cafe with a monthly changing selection of house beans. There are usually two single-origin options on the go – one prepared as espresso, the other as batch – as well as an excellent decaf.

🛈 INSIDER'S TIP
PAIR A BATCH BREW WITH A ROUND OF TOASTED SOURDOUGH AND WHIPPED MARMITE BUTTER

Birch's new brunch menu makes sticking around a tempting proposition. The pared-back line-up of seasonal dishes includes antipodean staples such as coconut bircher with stewed fruits and toasted nuts, and poached eggs with 'nudja, salted ricotta and salsa verde on sourdough.

If you're working your way around the island's coffee shops, you might be reunited with Birch's beans as Niall also supplies a number of indie cafes.

ESTABLISHED
2020

KEY ROASTER
Birch

BREWING METHOD
Espresso, filter

MACHINE
Slayer Steam LP

GRINDER
Mahlkonig EK43 S, Bentwood Vertical 63, Mahlkonig E65s GbW

OPENING HOURS
Tue–Sun
8am–5pm

Gluten FREE

BEANS AVAILABLE
INSTORE

birch-skye.co 07775 857520
f @BIRCH ◎ @birch_skye

7 CAFE SIA

Ford Road, Broadford, Isle of Skye, IV49 9AB

Coffee lovers entering the Isle of Skye by land should make a beeline for this roadside find that's just a stone's throw from the Skye Bridge. Standing in the shadow of the magnificent Red Cuillin mountains, Cafe Sia is the ultimate pit stop for a caffeine fix and bite to eat before heading into the island.

Roaster and barista Craig Steele sources beans from the team at Skye Coffee Roasters, who travel the short distance to drop off bags of their Sgitheanach blend and seasonal single-origin beans. Craig also roasts his own Cafe Sia blend, so visitors can choose between two Skye-bronzed blends for their first flat white of the trip.

INSIDER'S TIP: THOSE AFTER MELLOW RELAXATION SHOULD ASK FOR THEIR COFFEE LACED WITH A FEW DROPS OF CBD OIL

After 5pm, the cafe has more of a restaurant vibe when the island's only wood-fired pizza oven takes centre stage. The line-up of authentic Italian pizzas features creative Scottish toppings - try Over the Sea to Skye which is showered in seaweed, silverskin anchovies, Hebridean salmon, prawns, mussels and tomato.

Pair your pick of the slices with beers from Scottish breweries and end the night with a wee dram from the extensive whisky list.

ESTABLISHED
2014

KEY ROASTER
Skye Coffee Roasters

BREWING METHOD
Espresso

MACHINE
Fracino Contempo

GRINDER
Mahlkonig

OPENING HOURS
Mon–Sun
9am–9pm
(seasonal opening hours)

 Gluten FREE

 BEANS AVAILABLE INSTORE

 CYCLE FRIENDLY

 OUTDOOR seating

 DISABLED ACCESS

 BRING YOUR OWN Cup.

DOG FRIENDLY

cafesia.co.uk   01471 822616
f @cafesiaskye   🐦 @cafesiaskye   📷 @cafesia_skye

8 LEAN TO COFFEE

8 Ashaig, Isle of Skye, IV42 8PZ

Photo: Caroline McQuistin, Isle of Skye Media

A s its name suggests, this coffee shop (which operates out of a container and ancient croft house on the Isle of Skye) has a touch of the wild about it. Such is its rural island setting that, gazing through its windows at the vista, you could be forgiven for forgetting what you've ordered – until the smell of coffee brings you back to the serious business of breakfast.

Choose from a chia granola bowl, toastie or warm muffin to go with your espresso or filter. If you fancy one of the sourdough cardamom buns to pair with your brew, make sure you're at the front of the queue as they often sell out before they've even had a chance to cool down.

INSIDER'S TIP — CHECK OUT THE RANGE OF ALT HOT CHOCS AND MLKWRKS SUPERFOOD LATTES

Coffee is sourced from a rotating list of Scottish roasteries. The Lean To team like to operate at the sweet end of the spectrum, selecting beans with fruity or unusual tasting notes. However, if you have a real sweet tooth go for the honey-soaked chai latte.

Keep an eye on social media for seasonal opening hours and up-to-date info on the current beans in the hopper.

ESTABLISHED
2021

KEY ROASTER
Multiple
roasteries

BREWING METHOD
Espresso, filter

MACHINE
La Marzocco
Strada ABR

GRINDER
Mahlkonig E65s
GbW

OPENING HOURS
Fri–Tue
8am–3pm
(seasonal opening hours)

Gluten FREE

BEANS AVAILABLE
INSTORE

CYCLE FRIENDLY

OUTDOOR seating

BRING YOUR OWN Cup.

DOG FRIENDLY

f @leantocoffeeskye   @ @leantocoffee

9 SLAUGHTERHOUSE COFFEE

Marine Terrace North, Cromarty to Nigg ferry slipway, Cromarty, Highlands, IV11 8XZ

Adventurers setting off on a tour of the Highlands from Inverness will find some of the best coffee of their trip just a short drive from their starting point at this unassuming Cromarty coffee shop.

Located on the slipway of the Cromarty to Nigg ferry, Slaughterhouse has a spacious outside seating area and is hugely popular with roadtrippers seeking quality caffeine and the potential sighting of a dolphin in the firth. When the weather turns (this is the Highlands after all), there's also a cosy area inside where visitors can hunker down with coffee and a slice of cake from local producer Black Isle Baking.

🏷 REGULARS WHO TAKE A REUSABLE CUP GET THEIR TENTH COFFEE FREE

Whether choosing espresso or filter, locals and visitors can be assured that the beans will be phenomenally fresh as they're roasted next door by Vandyke Brothers Coffee. Its Tin Roof blend is the usual espresso choice of Slaughterhouse owner Laura Thompson, while batch brew and V60 options depend on which seasonal single-origins are being rustled up at the roastery.

ESTABLISHED
2017

KEY ROASTER
Vandyke Brothers Coffee

BREWING METHOD
Espresso, V60, batch brew

MACHINE
La Marzocco Linea PB

GRINDER
Mahlkonig EK43, Mahlkonig E65s GbW

OPENING HOURS
Thu–Mon
9am–3pm
(extended in summer)

 Gluten FREE

 BEANS AVAILABLE INSTORE

 CYCLE FRIENDLY

 OUTDOOR seating

 BRING YOUR OWN Cup

 DOG FRIENDLY

07809 446555
f @slaughterhousecoffee ◎ @slaughterhousecoffee

10 BATCHEN STREET COFFEE

33 Batchen Street, Elgin, Moray, IV30 1BH

Tourists might flock to the Moray Firth town of Elgin to sample drams at world-renowned whisky distilleries, but those after a caffeine hit make a beeline for Batchen Street Coffee. The speciality coffee shop has created quite a buzz around its top-notch beans and belly-busting breakfasts.

Whether you're after an espresso, V60 or Chemex, you're guaranteed quality single-origin coffee which has been roasted in-house by the Batchen Street team or locally by Cairngorm Leaf & Bean. Non-coffee drinkers can find satisfaction in infusions from Brew Tea Co. and Shibui Tea, and Bare Bones hot chocolate.

 INSIDER'S TIP MAKE LIKE A LOCAL AND ORDER THE PORK AND CHORIZO SAUSAGE ROLL

Go with an appetite as Batchen Street revels in a plethora of sweet and savoury breakfast options such as brioche french toast with crispy bacon, maple syrup and cinnamon, and breakfast naan stuffed with bacon, cream cheese, tomato and chilli chutney. Fans of the full Scottish brekkie will be swayed by the cafe's hunger-quashing bill of poached eggs, pork sausages, back bacon, haggis, roasted mushrooms and vine tomatoes.

ESTABLISHED
2017

KEY ROASTER
Batchen Street Coffee

BREWING METHOD
Espresso, Chemex, V60

MACHINE
La Marzocco Strada

GRINDER
Mahlkonig EK43, Macap MXD Xtreme

OPENING HOURS
Mon-Tue, Thu-Fri
9.30am–3pm
Sat
10am–4pm

 Gluten FREE

 BEANS AVAILABLE / INSTORE

 WIFI

 CYCLE FRIENDLY

 DISABLED ACCESS

 BRING YOUR OWN Cup

 DOG FRIENDLY

batchenstreetcoffee.uk 01343 545888
f @batchenstreetcoffee @batchenstreetcoffee

11 SPEYSIDE COFFEE ROASTING CO.

Kirk Cottage, South Road, Garmouth, Moray, IV32 7LU

Established in March 2017, Speyside Coffee Roasting Co. was the first SCA-qualified speciality coffee roastery in Moray. Located in the Speyside village of Garmouth, the hidden gem is popular with locals, walkers, cyclists and tourists in search of a great cup of coffee.

Based in the heart of single-malt whisky country, founders Grant and Jody Spence continue the single-origin theme in their coffee offering. Their roasting style focuses on quality and Grant keeps things simple with just three coffees on the bill: a medium-roast Brazilian, house decaf and a barrel-aged coffee produced in collaboration with Glen Moray Distillery in Elgin.

TURN YOUR PIT STOP INTO A STAY BY BOOKING THE ON-SITE SELF-CATERED ACCOMMODATION

Visit to sample the own-roasted coffee and stick around to tuck into freshly baked pastries, bacon rolls, toasted panini, scones and traybakes. If you're staying in the area, you'll likely come across Speyside Coffee beans again as Grant and Jody also supply other local indie cafes.

Pick up a souvenir of your trip from the cafe's retail shelves, which feature Speyside Coffee merch and locally produced gifts.

ESTABLISHED
2017

KEY ROASTER
Speyside Coffee Roasting Co.

BREWING METHOD
Espresso

MACHINE
Sanremo

GRINDER
Sanremo

OPENING HOURS
Wed–Sun
10am–3pm
(seasonal opening hours)

 Gluten FREE

 BEANS AVAILABLE INSTORE

 WIFI

 CYCLE FRIENDLY

 OUTDOOR SEATING

 DISABLED ACCESS

 BRING YOUR OWN CUP

 DOG FRIENDLY

speysidecoffee.co.uk   01343 870546

f @speysidecoffeeroastingco   🐦 @speysidecoffee   📷 @speysidecoffee

12 THE COFFEE APOTHECARY - ELLON

21 The Square, Ellon, Aberdeenshire, AB41 9JB

As day slips into night at this lively cafe, the shots of espresso pulled through the La Marzocco machine make their way into coupe glasses instead of ceramic cups.

The younger sibling of the original Coffee Apothecary in Udny, this Ellon outpost is open late four nights a week to serve food that's made for sharing (platters of cheese, charcuterie boards and nachos), alongside a curated list of cocktails, beers and non-alcoholic drinks. If you're planning a deep dive of the cocktail menu (the Espresso Martini is excellent) there are also heartier stomach-lining dishes such as slow-cooked beef lasagne and king prawn linguine.

 DRIVING? ASK WHICH KOMBUCHA IS CURRENTLY ON DRAFT

Of course, as the name implies, this is first and foremost a coffee shop and owners Jonny and Ali Aspden are self-professed speciality geeks. A reserve menu of frozen beans gives fellow fans the chance to sample rare coffees from a variety of different origins, prepared by Jonny and team as filter or espresso.

Further exploration can be found in the coffee flights. Choose from two different single-origin coffees side by side, the same coffee prepared as espresso and filter, or the same coffee as espresso and flat white.

ESTABLISHED
2019

KEY ROASTER
The Coffee Apothecary

BREWING METHOD
Espresso, Kalita Wave, cafetiere

MACHINE
La Marzocco Linea PB ABR

GRINDER
Mythos One, Mahlkonig EK43

OPENING HOURS
Mon–Tue
10am–4pm
Wed–Thu
10am–9pm
Fri–Sat
9am–10pm
Sun
9am–4pm

 Gluten FREE

 BEANS AVAILABLE INSTORE

 WIFI

 CYCLE FRIENDLY

 DISABLED ACCESS

 BRING YOUR OWN Cup.

 COFFEE COURSES

thecoffeeapothecary.co.uk   01358 721946

f @thecoffeeapothecaryellon   @thecoffeeapothecaryellon

13 THE COFFEE APOTHECARY – UDNY

Udny, Ellon, Aberdeenshire, AB41 7PQ

Once a bustling Aberdeenshire post office, The Coffee Apothecary is once more the epicentre of village life in Udny. Locals and visitors gather at the popular spot for expertly crafted coffee, homebaked cakes and friendly chat with the baristas.

Founders Jonny and Ali Aspden (who also run a second cafe in Ellon) are *'on a mission to make people fall in love with speciality coffee'*. As well as serving a sterling line-up of top-grade beans, they offer three masterclasses which cover filter coffee, espresso and latte art.

INSIDER'S TIP TREAT THE COFFEE LOVER IN YOUR LIFE TO A MASTERCLASS VOUCHER

Make the trip to watch the baristas work their magic, sample exciting coffees and tuck into tempting dishes such as fluffy pancakes laden with orange curd, sweet cream cheese and gingerbread crumb, and pork and black bean tacos.

Lockdown gave Jonny and Ali time to start working on a long-held dream: to add a Coffee Apothecary roastery to the mix. Following a successful crowdfunding campaign, work is underway on the customer-owned roastery (located behind the original cafe) which is due to start producing beans in early 2023. It will also house the popular masterclasses.

ESTABLISHED
2014

KEY ROASTER
The Coffee Apothecary

BREWING METHOD
Espresso, Kalita Wave, cafetiere

MACHINE
La Marzocco Linea PB ABR

GRINDER
Ceado E37T, Mahlkonig EK43

OPENING HOURS
Mon–Thu
10am–4pm
Fri–Sun
9am–4pm

 Gluten FREE

 BEANS AVAILABLE INSTORE

 WIFI

 CYCLE FRIENDLY

 OUTDOOR seating

 DISABLED ACCESS

 BRING YOUR OWN Cup

 COFFEE COURSES

thecoffeeapothecary.co.uk   01651 842253

f @thecoffeeapothecary @ @thecoffeeapothecary

14 DREAMY GOAT COFFEE CO.

Strathlene Cottage, North Street, Inverurie, Aberdeenshire, AB51 4DJ

The exterior of this Inverurie coffee shop might look like an unassuming residential property, but the endless stream of people heading through its doors and the hum of chatter from its courtyard picnic tables indicates that it's something altogether different.

Dreamy Goat was crowned Best Coffee House in the Scottish Cafe Awards 2022, so its team are known for knocking out best-in-show veggie brunches and gold-standard caffeine. Make a weekend visit for family-friendly smoothie bowls, pancake stacks and breakfast burritos paired with espresso and pourover options from local roastery Figment.

INSIDER'S TIP: VEGAN AND GLUTEN-FREE VISITORS WILL FIND LOTS OF OPTIONS ON THE INCLUSIVE MENUS

Mid-afternoon drop-ins will find a range of healthy snacks, including homemade bliss balls, flapjacks and thirst-quenching superfood smoothies.

Chef Michelle Rolfe and daughters took over the popular cafe in June 2022, and are upholding its reputation as a must-visit spot for brunch fans who won't compromise on coffee.

ESTABLISHED
2020

KEY ROASTER
Multiple roasteries

BREWING METHOD
Espresso, pourover, filter, batch brew

MACHINE
La Marzocco

GRINDER
Mythos One, Mahlkonig EK43

OPENING HOURS
Mon–Sun
10am–4pm

dreamygoatcoffee.com   01467 623220

f @dreamygoatcoffee @ @dreamygoatcoffee

15 FOODSTORY UNI

Taylor Building, Regent Walk, University of Aberdeen, Aberdeen, AB24 3EB

This coffee shop and lunch stop at University of Aberdeen was ahead of the game when it opened in 2018, becoming the first zero-packaging cafe in Scotland. Four years on, the eco-conscious team are just as fired up about their mission to cut waste and make speciality coffee as sustainable as possible.

Situated at the entrance to the law library, it's a hugely popular spot with students craving a caffeine hit before lectures or taking an hour out to enjoy a plant-centric lunch. Yet it's not just students who frequent the contemporary space: locals walking from town to Old Aberdeen also drop in for a stellar coffee and homemade bake from its bounteous counter.

 FORGOTTEN YOUR REUSABLE? BORROW ONE OF THE DONATED CUPS OR TUPPERWARE

Those looking to sharpen their mind ahead of a heavy study sesh can choose between the espresso roast from Obadiah in Edinburgh and the seasonal filter from guest Scottish roasteries such as Dear Green and Fortitude. Edible fuel comes in the form of stuffed focaccia, colourful salads and sourdough toasties.

ESTABLISHED
2018

KEY ROASTER
Obadiah

BREWING METHOD
Espresso, filter

MACHINE
La Marzocco Linea Classic

GRINDER
Mazzer

OPENING HOURS
Mon-Fri
8.30am-4pm

 Gluten FREE

 BEANS AVAILABLE INSTORE

 WIFI

 CYCLE FRIENDLY

 OUTDOOR SEATING

 DISABLED ACCESS

BRING YOUR OWN Cup

 DOG FRIENDLY

foodstorycafe.co.uk

f @thefoodstorycafe 🐦 @foodstorycoffee 📷 @foodstory.uni

16 FOODSTORY HUT

Beach Boulevard, Aberdeen, AB11 5DN

When this third Foodstory opened on Aberdeen Beach Esplanade in 2021, fans of the city institution were thrilled to find they could get their Foodstory fix with a side of sea views.

Not long after opening the takeaway hatch, the team expanded the hut so it could also house a micro-bakery, and the site is now a one-stop shop for excellent espresso and plant-based bakes. The house roast – a Mexican coffee from Dear Green in Glasgow – makes the perfect match for its Aberdeen-famous cinnamon buns (visit on the weekend when a speciality version of the bun takes the experience next-level).

 INSIDER'S TIP **CRAVING SOMETHING SAVOURY? CHECK OUT THE SOURDOUGH TOASTIES AND FOCACCIA SANDWICHES**

From this tiny space, resident baker Doireann crafts a host of tempting bakes. Peek inside the glass counter to spy what's available and choose between the likes of maple and pecan croissants, chocolate and orange pastries, and caramel and pecan croissant buns.

There's no seating inside the converted cargo-container, so pack a reusable and enjoy your spoils while taking a caffeinated stroll along the seafront.

ESTABLISHED
2021

KEY ROASTER
Dear Green
Coffee Roasters

BREWING METHOD
Espresso

MACHINE
La Marzocco
Linea Classic

GRINDER
Mazzer

OPENING HOURS
Mon-Sun
10am–3pm

 Gluten FREE

 BEANS AVAILABLE INSTORE

 CYCLE FRIENDLY

 OUTDOOR seating

 DISABLED ACCESS

 BRING YOUR OWN Cup

 DOG FRIENDLY

foodstorycafe.co.uk

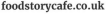 @thefoodstorycafe   @foodstorycoffee   @foodstoryscotland

17 FAFFLESS

47 Netherkirkgate, Aberdeen, AB10 1AU

You won't encounter any pomp or pretension at this art gallery and coffee, wine and premium-spirits bar. That's because, after experiencing snobbery at a wine fair in Edinburgh, owner Craig Thom decided to create his own relaxed space where customers could sip speciality-grade coffee, tuck into small plates and sample delicious drops without faff or formality.

Like the carefully curated artwork that lines the walls, coffee is treated as an art form at Faffless. The menu is extensive and the baristas friendly, so don't be shy to ask for recommendations and prep advice. Glasgow's Grain and Grind supply the house beans, but there are also guest filters from international roasteries such as Dak in the Netherlands and Japan's Single O.

 INSIDER'S TIP CHECK OUT THE SCHEDULE OF DRINKS TASTINGS, GALLERY EVENTS AND OPEN-MIC NIGHTS

Post 12pm, the coffee offering is supported by a tempting line-up of small plates and stronger sips. A fish-focused food menu features dishes such as squid and mint salad, sardine and rocket, and asparagoza (asparagus, mackerel and chilli). Pair your picks with one of the coffee cocktails – the Chocolate and Caramel Rumtini is the house speciality.

ESTABLISHED
2021

KEY ROASTER
Grain and Grind

BREWING METHOD
Espresso, AeroPress, Clever Dripper, cold brew

MACHINE
Astoria Rapallo

GRINDER
HeyCafé 2.0

OPENING HOURS
Wed–Sun
10am–11pm

 Gluten FREE

 BEANS AVAILABLE — INSTORE

 WIFI

 CYCLE FRIENDLY

 DISABLED ACCESS

 BRING YOUR OWN Cup

DOG FRIENDLY

fafflesscellar.com 07501 402373
@faffless_aberdeen

18 THE CULT OF COFFEE

28 Esslemont Avenue, Aberdeen, AB25 1SN

This pared-back coffee shop, tucked away on a quiet street in Aberdeen's city centre, is worth straying off the beaten track for.

Don't hunt down The Cult of Coffee for carefully curated brunch plates or fancy lunches, however, as the focus here is very much on the preparation of first-class speciality brews and delicious homemade cakes.

INSIDER'S TIP: ORDER A CAKE SLIDER (FIVE SLICES OF THE DAY'S BAKES) TO SHARE WITH FRIENDS

The CoC team have tapped into the fact that folk are increasingly swapping midday pints for flat whites, so this is a venue that perfectly pitches the 'coffee house as a social destination' vibe. Customers don't just pop in for a quick cup either: they stay a few hours to sample different beans and brewing options, with explanatory chat from the clued-up baristas.

Edinburgh's Artisan Roast is the main roaster on the menu, while the filter option is rotated every couple of weeks to entice regulars back for something new. Recent guest appearances include beans from New Ground, Manhattan and Hundred House.

On sunny afternoons, nab a table outside and soak up the rays. Take your pooch too: the CoC team love them.

ESTABLISHED
2017

KEY ROASTER
Artisan Roast
Coffee Roasters

BREWING METHOD
Espresso, V60,
batch brew,
Clever Dripper,
cold brew

MACHINE
La Marzocco
Linea PB

GRINDER
Mahlkonig
E80 Supreme,
Mahlkonig EK43

OPENING HOURS
Mon–Sat
8.30am–5pm
Sun
9am–5pm

 Gluten FREE

 BEANS AVAILABLE
 INSTORE

 WIFI

 OUTDOOR seating

 DISABLED ACCESS

 COFFEE COURSES

  DOG FRIENDLY

07793 406726
f @thecultofcoffee @the_cult_of_coffee

19 FOODSTORY

13-15 Thistle Street, Aberdeen, AB10 1XZ

When Sandy McKinnon and Lara Bishop established Foodstory in 2013 (the result of Scotland's first successful cafe crowdfunding campaign), they wanted to create a space where the people of Aberdeen could gather to feel connected as a community.

Their vision has turned into a resounding success and the cafe and events space on Thistle Street, along with sister venues at University of Aberdeen and Aberdeen Beach, have become legendary in the city.

 CHECK OUT SISTER ESTABLISHMENTS AT UNIVERSITY OF ABERDEEN AND ABERDEEN BEACH

'We love bringing people together,' says Sandy. *'Our aim is to provide a space where people feel safe and can switch off from the rest of the world.'*

If the primary focus is connectivity, the second is coffee. There are usually four beans on offer: a Mexican from Dear Green for milk-based espresso drinks, a Burundian from Obadiah for black espresso drinks, a Dear Green decaf and a rotating guest roast for filter.

A string of awards, including Best Coffee Shop at the BSA Hospitality Awards 2021, assures excellent execution. And, if you're looking for a sweet match for your brew, the homemade cinnamon buns are worth every second of the sugar crash that will inevitably follow.

ESTABLISHED
2013

KEY ROASTER
Dear Green
Coffee Roasters

BREWING METHOD
Espresso,
filter

MACHINE
La Marzocco
Linea PB

GRINDER
Victoria Arduino
Mythos One,
Mahlkonig
EK43, Mazzer
Luigi

OPENING HOURS
Mon
8.30am–3pm
Tue–Sat
8.30am–8pm
Sun
10am–3pm

foodstorycafe.co.uk

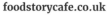 *@thefoodstorycafe*   *@foodstorycoffee*   *@foodstoryscotland*

20 FIGMENT

70 Countesswells Road, Aberdeen, AB15 7YJ

A 'life-changing' latte in Texas in 2012 was the catalyst for Neil Glover to trade his career in oil and gas for a fresh start in speciality coffee. The result was Figment, a cafe that combines his love of quality coffee with his desire to create a community space where people can relax and unwind.

The light and airy spot also houses the Figment roastery, which produces award-winning blends and a seasonal selection of single origins. Order the signature house roast, Wonderland, as a flat white to luxuriate in rich notes of caramel and chocolate.

 DROP IN ON FOOD-TRUCK FRIDAYS TO SAMPLE THE CITY'S LATEST STREET FOOD

Locals commune at the Countesswells Road venue for brunch as well as coffee. The menu changes throughout the year but you'll always find inventive dishes on offer. House favourites include freshly made cinnamon buns slathered in frosting, and the ultimate bacon roll served with scrambled eggs, hash browns and sriracha.

Beyond these daytime attractions, coffee fans should schedule an evening visit to sip wine and savour delicious small plates crafted using local ingredients.

ESTABLISHED
2018

KEY ROASTER
Figment Coffee Company

BREWING METHOD
Espresso, Kalita Wave, pourover, batch brew

MACHINE
Synesso MVP Hydra

GRINDER
Mahlkonig Peak

OPENING HOURS
Tue
10am–3pm
Wed–Thu, Sun
9am–4pm
Fri–Sat
9am–10pm

 Gluten FREE

 BEANS AVAILABLE INSTORE

 WIFI

CYCLE FRIENDLY

 OUTDOOR seating

 DISABLED ACCESS

 DOG FRIENDLY

figmentcoffee.com 01224 467500

f @figmentcoffee 🐦 @figmentcoffee 📷 @figmentcoffee

21 RIDE COFFEE HOUSE

46 Station Road, Banchory, Aberdeenshire, AB31 5YA

Wife and husband team Juliette and Simon Burnside combined their love of outdoor pursuits with a passion for quality coffee when they opened Ride Coffee House in 2018. A sister business to Simon's snow and skate store, Boarderline, the coffee shop attracts a steady stream of outdoor enthusiasts seeking speciality-grade caffeination.

Their needs are expertly met by Glasgow's Dear Green Coffee Roasters, while those looking for something a little different will revel in the luxury hot chocolates infused with Nutella and peppermint and topped with sky-high peaks of whipped cream. A good selection of cakes, soups and sandwiches supports the liquid line-up, and vegan and gluten-free options are available.

 ORDER A PORK AND BLACK PUDDING SAUSAGE ROLL – YOU WON'T REGRET IT

Spacious outdoor seating and bike racks make Ride a popular pit stop for mountain bikers traversing the trails at Scolty, as well as road cyclists passing through from Aberdeen.

Before you leave, pick up a jar of the house chutney. It's used in many of the cafe's recipes and is a tasty way to perk up a Sunday morning bacon buttie.

ESTABLISHED
2018

KEY ROASTER
Dear Green
Coffee Roasters

BREWING METHOD
Espresso

MACHINE
Conti CC100

GRINDER
Eureka Helios,
Ceado

OPENING HOURS
Mon–Sun
9am–5pm

01330 820946
f @ridecoffeehouse @ @ridecoffeehouse

22 BIRDHOUSE CAFE

74-76 High Street, Banchory, Aberdeenshire, AB31 5SS

When the pandemic left Ruth and Colin Redman stranded on the other side of the planet, they were struck hard by the antipodean coffee bug. The condition turned out to be permanent and, once able to migrate home to Scottish shores, resulted in them taking over Birdhouse Cafe in Banchory.

As new owners they wanted to do their own thing so, not content with merely serving the finest single-origin beans, they began roasting them too under the moniker Long Walk Coffee (named after a particularly stimulating stroll).

INSIDER'S TIP QUEUE EARLY TO KICKSTART YOUR WEEKEND WITH A LEGENDARY SATURDAY-MORNING CINNAMON SWIRL

As with the coffee, every delicious edible is created in-house including the sourdough. Ingredients are sourced as locally as possible and the breakfast, lunch and Sunday menus all feature gluten-free and plant-based options.

Within a year of landing in Aberdeenshire, the Birdhouse team racked up hundreds of five-star reviews. Locals now flock for grilled sourdough sandwiches, freshly baked cakes, takeaway treat boxes and afternoon teas served in recyclable and compostable packaging.

ESTABLISHED
2020

KEY ROASTER
Long Walk Coffee

BREWING METHOD
Espresso, V60, cold brew, AeroPress

MACHINE
Victoria Arduino Eagle One

GRINDER
Anfim

OPENING HOURS
Tue, Thu–Fri
8am–5pm
Wed
8am–2.30pm
Sat
9am–5pm
Sun
10am–4pm

 Gluten FREE

 BEANS AVAILABLE INSTORE

 WIFI

 CYCLE FRIENDLY

 DISABLED ACCESS

 BRING YOUR OWN Cup.

 COFFEE COURSES

DOG FRIENDLY

birdhousecafe.co.uk   01330 828456
 @birdhousecafe   @birdhousecafe2020

23 EH9 ESPRESSO

248-250 Perth Road, Dundee, DD1 4LL

Photo: Cameron Todd

Much like the Dundee art scene that inspires it, EH9's coffee line-up changes regularly to reflect the latest trends. Regulars are kept on their toes by its revolving curation, which includes at least two batch brews (updated up to three times a week), a weekly single-origin espresso and the Cairngorm house roast.

The team's relaxed and fluid approach to coffee sums up the EH9 experience. It's a fun, bright, pastel-hued space that has been designed by owner Fraser Smith to make everyone feel welcome and to evoke feelings of positivity. People of all generations pop in for a cuppa, but it's particularly beloved by the students and creatives who spill out of Dundee's contemporary arts school nearby.

 FOLLOW EH9 ESPRESSO ON TIKTOK FOR A FUN SNAPSHOT OF LIFE AT THE CAFE

Reflecting the times, EH9 taps into the Gen Z desire for social spaces that aren't centred around alcohol. The cafe attracts a post-work crowd for late-night socials and often hosts events. A recent example was a streetwear pop-up that raised money for those impacted by the war in Ukraine.

ESTABLISHED
2021

KEY ROASTER
Cairngorm Coffee

BREWING METHOD
Espresso,
batch brew

MACHINE
La Marzocco
Linea Classic

GRINDER
Victoria Arduino
Mythos One,
Mahlkonig EK43

OPENING HOURS
Mon–Sun
9am–6pm
(seasonal opening hours)

 Gluten FREE

 BEANS AVAILABLE INSTORE

 WIFI

 DISABLED ACCESS

 BRING YOUR OWN Cup

 DOG FRIENDLY

07566 222475
@eh9.espresso

24 SPOILED LIFE

15 Greyfriars Gardens, St Andrews, Fife, KY16 9HG

Pop into Spoiled Life for a quick coffee and there's a good chance you'll leave several hours later than planned with a full stomach and bag overflowing with prints, t-shirts and gorgeous homewares.

Set over two levels with a spiral staircase at its core, the lifestyle store, clothing shop and coffee house has everything the design-led caffeinista could desire. Browse environmentally conscious fashion brands, flick through indie magazines and pick up items to dress your home from the curation of candles, cushions, cups and more.

💡 INSIDER'S TIP
CHECK SOCIAL FOR EVENTS SUCH AS JAZZ NIGHTS, EVENING SHOPPING AND DJ SETS

Then take a seat on the mezzanine and watch the other shoppers as you sip a perfectly poured flat white. Or head up to the coffee bar to see the baristas in action. Beans from The Roasting Project in Burntisland fill the hoppers and are paired with locally sourced milk in a range of espresso-based drinks.

Treat yourself to a slice of one of the cakes or a flaky pastry from local bakeries. Flavours change weekly and include vegan and gluten-free options.

ESTABLISHED
2020

KEY ROASTER
The Roasting Project

BREWING METHOD
Espresso, V60

MACHINE
La Spaziale S5
EK Compact

GRINDER
Anfim Pratica

OPENING HOURS
Mon, Wed–Sat
9am–6pm
Sun
10am–5pm

 Gluten FREE

 BEANS AVAILABLE INSTORE

 WIFI

 OUTDOOR seating

 BRING YOUR OWN cup

 DOG FRIENDLY

spoiledlife.co.uk   01334 487187

f @spoiledlifestore   ◎ @spoiledlifestore

25 THE ROASTING PROJECT

253a High Street, Burntisland, Fife, KY3 9AQ

When brothers Mark and Gary Braid opened The Roasting Project in 2018, they not only established a coffee shop and micro-roastery, they also created a community hub for the people of Burntisland.

Their house blend, Project X, is the perennial favourite among regulars who stop by for a coffee and a catch-up. It's bolstered by an assortment of single origins and a coffee called Dark Matter – a blend of Colombian and Mexican beans paired in response to customer demand for a darker roast. Order it to experience its winning combination of blackcurrant, honey and bakewell-tart flavours.

INSIDER'S TIP JOIN THE PROJECT'S COFFEE CLUB TO GET THE LATEST SEASONAL COFFEES DELIVERED TO YOUR DOOR

Roasting duties are overseen by head of coffee Clare, but the entire team are happy to give customers the intel on how the beans have travelled from farm to cup. They're also good at recommending the best prep methods for each coffee.

Plan an extended visit to sample the brunch menu which includes the likes of Bombay eggs (fried eggs served with sourdough, mango chutney, chimichurri, yogurt and chilli seeds) and staples such as the TRP reuben and brioche stack.

ESTABLISHED
2018

KEY ROASTER
The Roasting Project

BREWING METHOD
Espresso, V60, batch brew, AeroPress, cafetiere

MACHINE
Slayer Steam X

GRINDER
Mahlkonig Peak, Mahlkonig EK43

OPENING HOURS
Wed–Sun
10am–3.30pm

Gluten FREE

BEANS AVAILABLE INSTORE

WIFI

CYCLE FRIENDLY

OUTDOOR seating

DISABLED ACCESS

BRING YOUR OWN Cup

theroastingproject.co.uk   01592 873680
@theroastingproject   @theroastingproject

26 HBW COFFEE

54-56 Barnton Street, Stirling, FK8 1NA

While studying in America, HBW founder Conor was so inspired by the community spirit of its independent coffee scene that, on returning home to Stirling, he opened a cafe of his own.

Conor's original inspiration is evident as soon as you set eyes on HBW. From the diner-style signage to the red, white and blue colour scheme, the sociable space is an ode to American cafe culture.

 INSIDER'S TIP FOR A SWEET FIX, ORDER A VEGAN WHITE HOT CHOCOLATE

The spirit of the States also extends to the exclusively vegan and feelgood food menu. Pancakes and doughnuts are sought-after accompaniments to steaming cups of batch brew, while breakfast plates include Stateside staples such as burritos stuffed with spicy barbecue beans, scrambled tofu, cream cheese, spinach and burrito sauce.

From a gleaming La Marzocco, Conor and his barista crew crank out a gold-star selection of espresso drinks using beans from Scottish roasteries such as The Good Coffee Cartel, Glen Lyon and Manifesto. There are batch brew options too – ask about the day's line-up.

ESTABLISHED
2018

KEY ROASTER
Multiple roasteries

BREWING METHOD
Espresso, batch brew

MACHINE
La Marzocco Linea FB70

GRINDER
Ceado E37T, Mahlkonig EK43

OPENING HOURS
Wed–Sun
10am–4pm

 Gluten FREE

 BEANS AVAILABLE INSTORE

 WIFI

 CYCLE FRIENDLY

 OUTDOOR SEATING

 DISABLED ACCESS

 BRING YOUR OWN Cup

 DOG FRIENDLY

hbwcoffee.co.uk   **01786 451973**
f @hbwcoffee   @hbwcoffee

AREA

1

ROASTERIES

27 TEMPLE HARRIS COFFEE ROASTERS

22 Northton, Isle of Harris, Outer Hebrides, HS3 3JA

This micro-roastery in the Outer Hebrides is an exciting new addition to the Scottish speciality scene.

The Temple cafe, deli and bakery has been a hero spot on the Isle of Harris since 2019, winning over visitors with its great coffee and food menus stuffed with seasonal ingredients grown on its own croft. In 2022, the team upped its appeal yet further by taking the leap into roasting their own coffee.

'THE TEAM FOLLOWED THE PRINCIPLES OF PERFUMERY IN THE CREATION OF THEIR SEASONAL ESPRESSO BLEND'

Setting up a roastery in the Outer Hebrides is no mean feat (the roaster took over a year to reach the island), but the 12kg Probat now chugs away full-time, cooking up an ever-evolving range of single origins, which have been sourced by trading partner Falcon.

In the creation of the Temple Seasonal Espresso blend, the team (which includes a former distilling perfumer) followed the principles of perfumery: the coffees are categorised into top, heart and base notes, and then blended for balance and exciting flavours.

Want to visit IRL? Get the most from your Temple trip by joining a cupping sesh, sticking around for one of the cocktail evenings or, at the very least, chasing your pick of the coffee menu with a deliciously sticky machair bun.

ESTABLISHED
2022

ROASTER MAKE & SIZE
Probat 12kg

CAFE ONSITE

OPEN TO THE PUBLIC

BEANS AVAILABLE

templeharris.com   07979 926831
f @temple 🐦 @thetempleharris 📷 @thetempleharris

28 VANDYKE BROTHERS COFFEE

The Old Slaughterhouse, George Street, Cromarty, Highlands, IV11 8XZ

Housed in a former slaughterhouse on the tip of the Black Isle and overlooking the Cromarty Firth, this roastery is about as far from the coffee-quaffing metropolis as it's possible to be.

Yet, despite this rural setting, the small-batch roastery has built a solid rep across Scotland and beyond for its plethora of Highlands coffees. The line-up includes the recent Great Taste award winner Colombia El Vergel 'Guavabanana', which combines the sweet, fulsome flavours of forest fruits with a subtle umami finish.

'CUSTOMERS BENEFIT FROM A HANDS-ON PARTNERSHIP WITH THE ROASTERY'

Head roaster Tony Vandyke, who honed his coffee skills down under, focuses on coffee quality rather than buying beans from any one specific region. He says: *'We get coffee from wherever takes our interest, based on quality and taste. We regularly source from Brazil, Colombia, Guatemala, Ethiopia, Peru, Democratic Republic of the Congo, Panama and Yemen.'*

Aside from receiving consistently top-notch beans, customers also benefit from a hands-on partnership with the roastery: the VBC team oversee all aspects including selection and installation of machinery, and barista training (both on-site and at the roastery) to further polish customers' coffee-making skills.

ESTABLISHED
2016

ROASTER MAKE & SIZE
Probat P5 5kg
Ikawa Pro

OPEN
BY APPOINTMENT

BEANS
AVAILABLE

vandykebrothers.co.uk   07494 492695
@ *@vandykebros*

29 MAISON DIEU COFFEE ROASTERS

Old Sonoco Buildings, Montrose Street, Brechin, Angus, DD9 7RU

Professional footballer to coffee roaster isn't a conventional career path, yet it was the route that friends Euan Spark and John Souttar embarked on when they established Maison Dieu in 2020.

While taking a break from football due to injury, John (who still plays for Scotland) decided it was the right time to follow his dream of roasting speciality coffee and teamed up with friend and fellow pro footballer Euan. Once they'd found their perfect venue, they made a series of trips to The Scottish Barista Academy in Livingston where Jim Watson taught them to roast coffee.

'VISITORS CAN DROP BY TO TASTE THE LATEST BATCH'

Two years on, Maison Dieu is a fully functioning roastery and coffee shop. Euan heads up the roasting operation and uses a 10kg Toper to craft a seasonal selection of single origins from traceable farms in Central America. Locals and visitors drop by to taste the latest batch at the brew bar or sip their pick in the garden.

Sustainability is a priority for the duo, so all of the coffee bags used are recyclable (customers can even bring them back to the roastery). Wholesale customers receive beans in reusable tubs.

ESTABLISHED
2020

ROASTER MAKE & SIZE
Toper 10kg

OPEN
TO THE PUBLIC

COFFEE
COURSES

BEANS
AVAILABLE

maisondieucoffee.co.uk   **07446 873079**
f @maisondieucoffee ⊙ @maisondieucoffee

30 SACRED GROUNDS COFFEE COMPANY

Unit 15 Arbroath Business Centre, 31 Dens Road, Arbroath, Angus, DD11 1RS

While the focus at Sacred Grounds will always be on producing single-origin coffees of the finest quality, founders Kathryn, Jamie and Ian like to shake things up every now and then with the release of a limited-edition blend.

Following the success of their festive Another Bloomin' Christmas Blend, the trio were inspired to continue creating bespoke seasonal creations.

'We work to enhance the flavour of blends by using the unique profiles of our single-origin coffees. They're fun to develop and bring another element to our offering,' says Kathryn.

The team have recently collaborated with local festival Beer & Berries in the production of a genre-bending creation. The Beer & Berries Blend marries the bold malty notes of beer with the fruitiness of berries and the result is an unusual, and delicious, coffee.

'THE TRIO WERE INSPIRED TO CONTINUE CREATING BESPOKE SEASONAL CREATIONS'

Chief roaster Jamie is responsible for these innovative blends, cooking them up on a 5kg Toper (called Fatima) at the roastery on the banks of the Brothock Burn.

ESTABLISHED
2015

ROASTER MAKE & SIZE
Toper 5kg

OPEN
BY APPOINTMENT

BEANS
AVAILABLE

sacred-grounds.coffee   07808 806610

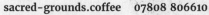
f @sacredgroundscoffeecompany 🐦 @sacredgrounds14 📷 @sacred_grounds_coffee_company

IT STARTS WITH COFFEE BERRIES...

A great deal of love, care, and attention goes into these wonderful little things. Altitude, precipitation, soil, climate, shade; all to nourish one little bean. But in this state; it's not drinkable. It's not tasty. It's not complex. It's not ready.

But it has potential. Before it becomes a delicious pour over, someone needs to process, roast, package, brew, and serve your bean. This is where a whole other world of skill, creativity, experience, and technical know-how comes into play.

This is what we do with your business. You grow it. You tend to it. You care for it. We're a speciality marketing agency who take your business, work our magic, and serve it to your customers. We are Story Shop. How about a coffee?

@wearestoryshop
wearestoryshop.com

31 THE BEAN SHOP

67 George Street, Perth, Perthshire, PH1 5LB

Nineteen years ago, John and Lorna Bruce decided to turn their passion for coffee into a full-time business and have been rolling out the finest speciality beans ever since.

Based in a charming little store opposite Perth Museum and Art Gallery, The Bean Shop contains a cornucopia of blends, single origins and coffee paraphernalia. Beans are available to buy by weight, so visitors can select a pick 'n' mix of coffees to sample at home.

The pair source their greens from across the Americas, Africa and Asia via a bank of trusted importers. Once the beans land in Perth, they're roasted in small batches to ensure optimum freshness. As roasters (as well as retailers), the team are always up for helping customers with questions and queries, so don't be afraid to get experimental with your choices. Regular visitors also get to take advantage of the loyalty scheme, which offers discounts on purchases.

'VISITORS CAN SELECT A PICK 'N' MIX OF COFFEES TO SAMPLE AT HOME'

If you can't visit The Bean Shop in person, its well-stocked website – plus subscription options for weekly, fortnightly or monthly coffee drops – should hit the mark. Gift subscriptions are also available.

ESTABLISHED
2003

ROASTER MAKE & SIZE
Probat 5kg
Loring 15kg
Probat 25kg
IKAWA

OPEN
BY APPOINTMENT

COFFEE
COURSES

BEANS
AVAILABLE

thebeanshop.co.uk   **01738 449955**
f @thebeanshopuk   🐦 @thebeanshopuk   📷 @thebeanshopuk

32 THE ROASTING PROJECT

253a High Street, Burntisland, Fife, KY3 9AQ

There's no doubt that the focus at this family-run roastery is on flavour. The Roasting Project team are inspired by coffee's infinite possibilities and enjoy nothing more than unlocking fresh flavour profiles.

To unearth novel notes, they fire up their 5kg Diedrich roaster (called Big June) and carefully select complementary lots to create unique coffees.

'THE TEAM ARE INSPIRED BY COFFEE'S INFINITE POSSIBILITIES'

The process has resulted in flavour-bomb blends such as The Black Rock (Brazilian, Guatemalan and Colombian beans) which sings of Maltesers, jam, candied fruit and toffee, as well as lighter creations like Homebrew (Peruvian, Guatemalan and Ethiopian beans) which promises notes of raspberry, pineapple, marshmallow and puff candy (AKA cinder toffee).

There's no better place to roadtest TRP's funky roasts – which include anaerobically fermented, decaffeinated and infused beans – than at its adjoining coffee shop. The cafe-roastery has been visited by First Minister Nicola Sturgeon, who learnt the art of slinging 'spros and slurped some top-tier coffee when she stopped by.

ESTABLISHED
2019

ROASTER MAKE & SIZE
Diedrich
IR-5 5kg

CAFE ONSITE

OPEN TO THE PUBLIC

COFFEE COURSES

BEANS AVAILABLE

theroastingproject.co.uk   01592 873680
f @theroastingproject   @theroastingproject

33 STIRLING COFFEE

8 King Street, Stirling, FK8 1AY

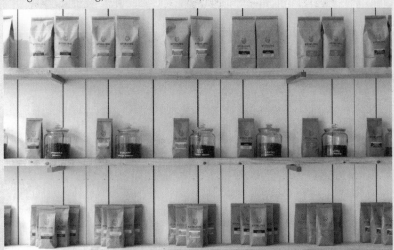

I f you're in Stirling and spy the Stirling Coffee wolf emblem swinging from the roastery shopfront, don't miss the opportunity to replenish your home haul of speciality beans.

You'll be greeted by a knowledgeable team who love to guide customers through their range of single-origin coffees. Let the experts match a roast to your taste, or enjoy exploring the wall-to-wall selection and give something new a whirl.

'A SWEET EL SALVADORAN COFFEE WITH NOTES OF CITRUS, VANILLA AND RICH CHOCOLATE'

The team source from across the coffee-growing belt to curate an exciting selection of beans to experiment with. The Central American selection receives particular praise from the roastery's fans and includes a sweet El Salvadoran coffee with notes of citrus, vanilla and rich chocolate.

If you can't visit the roastery shop IRL (it's open Mondays to Saturdays), head to its website where all of the roasts are listed and ready to be ordered. Each bag of beans is roasted within two days of mailing for ultimate freshness. There's also a subscription service that will keep you well caffeinated on a regular basis.

ESTABLISHED
2018

ROASTER MAKE & SIZE
Ambex 15kg
Ambex 5kg

BEANS AVAILABLE

OPEN TO THE PUBLIC

stirlingcoffee.co.uk   01786 357577
f @stirlingcoffee @stirling.coffee

AREA

2

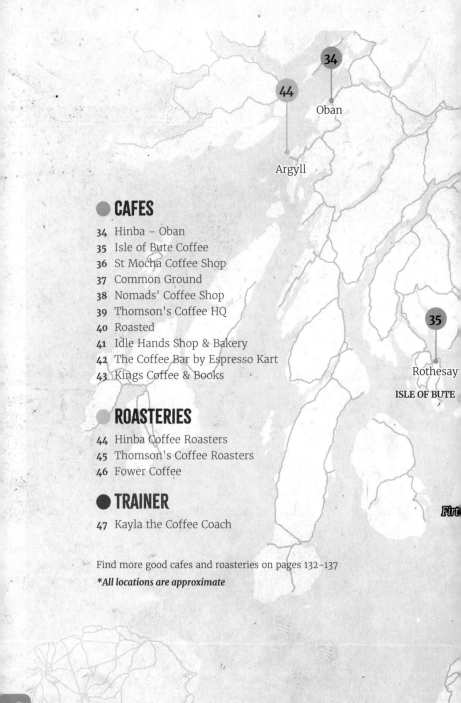

34
44
Oban
Argyll

CAFES

ROASTERIES

TRAINER

35
Rothesay

ISLE OF BUTE

Firt

Find more good cafes and roasteries on pages 132–137

All locations are approximate

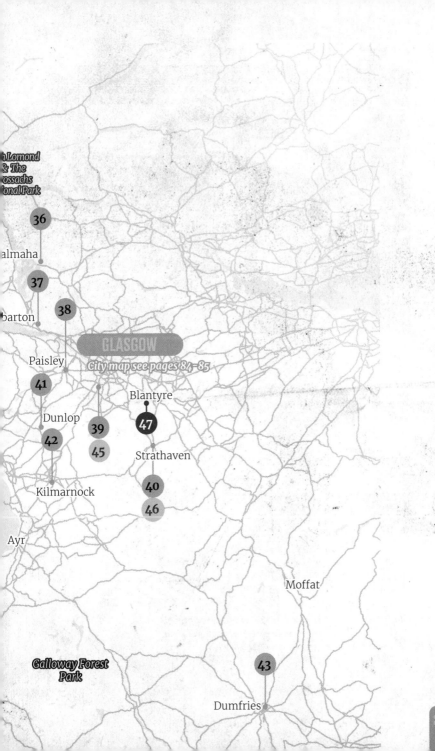

Loch Lomond
& The
Trossachs
National Park

36

Balmaha

37

Dumbarton

38

GLASGOW
City map see pages 84–85

Paisley

Blantyre

41

Dunlop

39

47

42

45

Strathaven

Kilmarnock

40

46

Ayr

Moffat

Galloway Forest
Park

43

Dumfries

34 HINBA – OBAN

62 George Street, Oban, Argyll, PA34 5SD

Hinba founders Fergus McCoss and Ness Achilles travelled the world before returning to their Scottish roots to establish a roastery on the unsullied Isle of Seil and this charming sister cafe on the beautiful west coast of Scotland.

The pair's passion for coffee is matched only by their commitment to Fairtrade and sustainability. All of the speciality coffee served as espresso or batch brew at this George Street venue is carefully sourced and then roasted at the in-house roastery.

 INSIDER'S TIP **VISIT IN THE EVENING FOR SPANISH SMALL PLATES AND A SELECTION OF LOCAL GINS**

Visitors to Hinba's Oban outpost (find a second cafe on Glasgow's Dumbarton Road) have a revolving selection of single origins to choose from, sourced from Central and South America. Pair your pick with a pastry or empanada from the selection of foodie bites.

Riffing on the name Hinba, Fergus and Ness recently added a gin bar to the shop. Extended opening hours (Thursdays to Sundays) enable patrons to sample a wide range of Scottish gins, craft beers and wines.

ESTABLISHED
2020

KEY ROASTER
Hinba Coffee Roasters

BREWING METHOD
Espresso, batch brew

MACHINE
Astoria Gloria

GRINDER
Compak F8

OPENING HOURS
Mon–Sun
9am–4pm
Thu–Sun
5pm–9.30pm

 Gluten FREE

 BEANS AVAILABLE INSTORE

 OUTDOOR SEATING

 DISABLED ACCESS

 BRING YOUR OWN CUP

 DOG FRIENDLY

hinba.co.uk   **07956 734913**
f @hinba.coffee.roasters   @hinba.coffee.roasters

35 ISLE OF BUTE COFFEE

10 Castle Street, Rothesay, Isle of Bute, PA20 9HA

If you're embarking on a coffee tour of Scotland, don't write off this new venue just because you'll need to venture across the Firth of Clyde to the Isle of Bute: the island is one of the country's most accessible and only a short ferry ride from Wemyss Bay.

In 2022, with the help of Lisa Lawson of Dear Green Coffee Roasters in Glasgow, Mhairi Mackenzie opened Bute's first speciality brew bar within her jewellery shop Bonnie Bling. The setting makes for a unique coffee experience: a sensory mash-up of kaleidoscopic jewellery twinkling from the shelves, the hiss of the Conti machine and the waft of freshly ground beans.

 PICK UP A BAG OF THE ISLE OF BUTE COFFEE BLEND AS A SOUVENIR FROM YOUR TRIP

Lisa (who was born on the island) worked with Mhairi to create a bespoke Isle of Bute Coffee blend, a delicious mix of Colombian and Brazilian beans. It's roasted for both espresso and filter, so you can sample it in your preferred brew style.

A short and sweet food offering keeps the coffee company, including island-made bakes, sourdough toast and the delicious treat of smoked salmon from Scotland's oldest working smokehouse.

ESTABLISHED
2022

KEY ROASTER
Dear Green
Coffee Roasters

BREWING METHOD
Espresso, filter

MACHINE
Conti CC202

GRINDER
Compak E6

OPENING HOURS
Mon–Tue,
Thu–Sat
9am–3pm

 Gluten FREE

 BEANS AVAILABLE INSTORE

 WIFI

 CYCLE FRIENDLY

 OUTDOOR seating

 DISABLED ACCESS

 BRING YOUR OWN Cup

DOG FRIENDLY

butecoffee.com
f @isleofbutecoffee @isleofbutecoffee

36 ST MOCHA COFFEE SHOP

Main Street, Balmaha, Loch Lomond, Glasgow, G63 0JQ

For decades, people have visited Loch Lomond and The Trossachs for the awe-inspiring scenery and picturesque walks. Now they can add National Park-roasted artisan coffee and homemade ice cream to their list of reasons to make a trip.

Brothers Stuart and David Fraser have served top-notch beans at St Mocha since 2014, but, in 2017, they decided to take their passion for quality caffeine a step further and add a roasting wing to the coffee shop. Guests can now sip impeccably smooth home-roasted brews while listening to the rhythmic hum of the Giesen roaster next door.

 INSIDER'S TIP **CHECK OUT SISTER VENUES THE STATION IN ABERFOYLE AND THE ST MOCHA DRIVE-THRU IN CARBETH**

Ice cream may not have the coffee-pairing reputation of cakes and bakes but the brothers' homemade gelato is an obvious match to a crema-rich espresso – whatever the weather. There's also a menu of meaty, veggie and vegan snacks to fortify body and soul before taking a bracing lochside walk.

ESTABLISHED
2014

KEY ROASTER
Loch Lomond Coffee Co.

BREWING METHOD
Espresso

MACHINE
La Marzocco Linea PB

GRINDER
Mazzer Kold

OPENING HOURS
Mon–Sun
8.30am–6pm
(seasonal opening hours)

 Gluten FREE

 BEANS AVAILABLE / INSTORE

 WIFI

 CYCLE FRIENDLY

 OUTDOOR SEATING

 DISABLED ACCESS

 BRING YOUR OWN CUP

stmocha.co.uk   01360 870357
f @stmocha ◎ @stmochacoffee

37 COMMON GROUND

171 Glasgow Road, East Dumbarton Station, Dumbarton, G82 1DN

Commuters alighting at Dumbarton East train station are greeted by the heavenly aroma of freshly ground coffee beans emanating from this little cafe tucked beneath a railway bridge.

As the only speciality find in Dumbarton, Common Ground attracts more than just travellers passing through the station and has become an in-the-know fave for locals.

 INSIDER'S TIP CHECK INSTAGRAM FOR THE LATEST WEEKEND FOCACCIA SPECIAL

New owners Franco and Esther took over in 2022 and have enjoyed taking the coffee offering up a notch. With creds including ten years of experience working in coffee shops across the world, they love showcasing the best of Scotland's roaring roasting scene at this new venture.

Esther looks after the short-and-sweet food offering, which is inspired by her German heritage. Everything – from the daily sourdough sandwiches through to the weekend specials and cinnamon buns – is made from scratch each morning.

There are a few seats for those who want to stick around to enjoy the spoils and chat to Franco about the latest espresso in the hopper, but, for most, this is a grab-and-go spot.

ESTABLISHED
2020

KEY ROASTER
Naked Roaster Coffee

BREWING METHOD
Espresso, batch brew

MACHINE
La Marzocco Linea Classic

GRINDER
Mahlkonig E65s

OPENING HOURS
Tue–Fri
7am–3pm
Sat–Sun
9am–3pm

 BEANS AVAILABLE INSTORE

 BRING YOUR OWN Cup

 DOG FRIENDLY

f @commongrounddumbarton   @common_ground_dumbarton

GREAT COFFEE SHOPS DESERVE GREAT CAKE.

@cakesmiths.h[o]

38 NOMADS' COFFEE SHOP

63 High Street, Paisley, Renfrewshire, PA1 2AS

This Paisley coffee shop opened in the town's West End in 2021 and has become a popular haunt for students and discerning locals looking for a quality brew.

Owners Charlotte and Amit Biswas took on the 19th-century building before the pandemic and spent the lockdowns lovingly restoring it. Curved glass, decorative tiles and a giant street clock on the exterior brickwork showcase the cafe's resplendent history.

 WANT TO UP YOUR COFFEE GAME? BOOK A SPOT AT ONE OF THE REGULAR CUPPING COURSES

Decor aside, the focus is on educating the people of Paisley about the value and joy to be found in speciality coffee. Drop in for a spot of coffee theatre, where filter drinks are brewed at the table while the kilted barista explains the process. Or book one of Nomads' coffee courses to learn how to get the most from your beans at home.

Provenance is important to the couple who travelled across the world to learn about the coffee-growing industry.

'Coffee farmers in countries such as Colombia and Ethiopia often struggle to feed their families, as profits go to the middleman and big corporate companies. We wanted to do something that respected the people who grow the coffee,' says Amit.

ESTABLISHED
2021

KEY ROASTER
Nuach Coffee Roasters

BREWING METHOD
Espresso, AeroPress, V60, syphon

MACHINE
La Marzocco Linea PB

GRINDER
Compak

OPENING HOURS
Mon–Sat
8am–5pm
Sun
9.30am–4.30pm

 Gluten FREE

 BEANS AVAILABLE INSTORE

 WIFI

 CYCLE FRIENDLY

 OUTDOOR Seating

 DISABLED ACCESS

 BRING YOUR OWN Cup

 COFFEE COURSES

 DOG FRIENDLY

nomadscoffee.co.uk   01418 875066

f @nomadscoffeeshop @nomadscoffeeshop

39 THOMSON'S COFFEE HQ

211 Fenwick Road, Giffnock, East Renfrewshire, G46 6JD

There's something very special about drinking own-roasted coffee served by seasoned pros on their own turf. And that's just what you get when you visit Thomson's Coffee HQ, which is just under a mile from the roastery.

The 180-year-old company's new hub is a former bank, which combines its offices and retail showroom with an inviting cafe experience. The industrial wood, stone and steel setting is bejewelled with brewing paraphernalia and Thomson's branded goods and beans. Regularly rotating self-service silos are stocked with three coffees from the house collection and available whole or ground-to-order for home brewing.

INSIDER'S TIP POINT EIGHT ESPRESSO IS NAMED AFTER THE 0.8 MILES IT HAS TRAVELLED FROM ROASTERY TO CUP

When it comes to sampling the goods, there's no better place to taste-test Thomson's Glasgow-roasted blends and single origins. Beans from across the coffee-growing belt are prepared as espresso and batch brew, and best accompanied by something flaky from the team's new bakery (a collaboration with local indie Short Long Black).

ESTABLISHED
2022

KEY ROASTER
Thomson's
Coffee Roasters

BREWING METHOD
Espresso,
batch brew

MACHINE
Victoria Arduino
Eagle One

GRINDER
Victoria Arduino
Mythos MY75,
Bentwood

OPENING HOURS
Mon, Wed-Fri
7.30am-4.30pm
Sat-Sun
9am-4.30pm

Gluten FREE

BEANS AVAILABLE
INSTORE

WIFI

DISABLED ACCESS

BRING YOUR OWN cup

DOG FRIENDLY

thomsonscoffee.com
@thomsons.hq

40 ROASTED

41 Common Green, Strathaven, South Lanarkshire, ML10 6AQ

This cafe-bakery in the Lanarkshire town of Strathaven is as celebrated for its super-stacked toasties as it is for its flat whites.

The Mac Daddy (a symphony of macaroni cheese, black pudding, mozzarella and mustard, layered between thick slices of house sourdough) and the Gyros Queen (harissa lamb, lemon-roasted potatoes, tomato, red onion and tzatziki on homemade pitta) are just two of the eye-widening specials. Add to that a counter laden with pies, sausage rolls, spanakopita and other pastries and you can understand why Roasted is always packed out.

 THE BRISKET TOASTIE WITH SRIRACHA MAYO IS A CONSISTENT CROWD-PLEASER

The man crafting this inventive menu is chef owner Theo Giameos, an Australian with proud Greek heritage, who is as passionate about coffee as he is about pastry. For the house beans Theo has chosen the Bronco blend from The Good Coffee Cartel in Glasgow, which packs a chocolatey hazelnut punch as espresso and pourover.

The vibe here is rustic – plywood walls, exposed shelves and industrial-style lighting – but what it might lack in cosy comfort it certainly makes up for in banging brews and an above-par lunch line-up.

ESTABLISHED
2018

KEY ROASTER
The Good Coffee Cartel

BREWING METHOD
Espresso, V60, batch brew

MACHINE
Conti MC Ultima

GRINDER
Anfim SCODY II

OPENING HOURS
Wed–Sat
9am–3pm

roastedstrathaven.co.uk   07926 259399
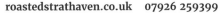 @roastedstrathaven   @roastedtheo   @roastedstrathaven

41 IDLE HANDS SHOP & BAKERY

44 Main Street, Dunlop, East Ayrshire, KA3 4AN

Tucked away in a scenic village, this European-style bakery and shop is a perfect drop-in for cyclists, walkers or anyone wanting top-notch refreshment that's a little out of the ordinary.

Contrary to its name, there's nothing idle about the hands that work in this perennially popular spot. And it's not just the pleasing selection of cakes and pastries that keeps the customers coming back for more, it's also the team's commitment to quality and passion for presentation.

INSIDER'S TIP CHECK SOCIAL FOR POP-UP EVENTS SUCH AS CANNOLI DAY, DOUGHNUT AND COFFEE EVENINGS, AND ICE-CREAM NIGHTS

Complementing the on-point patisserie and colourful creations is speciality coffee from Mokaflor in Florence. The line-up of espresso drinks are ground by a Mazzer, extracted on a Gaggia and poured into perfect flat whites by dextrous baristas.

The coffee beans used are available in the adjoining shop, along with tasty savouries such as spanakopita, sausage rolls, veggie tartlets and a variety of delicious breads. You'll also find artisanal products not easily available elsewhere, plus soft-serve ice cream and sorbet.

ESTABLISHED
2019

KEY ROASTER
Mokaflor

BREWING METHOD
Espresso

MACHINE
Gaggia

GRINDER
Mazzer

OPENING HOURS
Thu, Sun
11am–3pm
Fri
11am–4pm
Sat
10am–4pm

idlehandsshop.co.uk   **07479 490172**
f @idlehandsdunlop @idlehandsdunlop

42 THE COFFEE BAR BY ESPRESSO KART

43 Campbell Place, Riccarton, Kilmarnock, East Ayrshire, KA1 4DY

The Espresso Kart is a speciality coffee van beloved across Ayrshire for bringing excellent espresso to school fairs, farmers' markets and corporate shindigs.

When the pandemic hit, owner Stuart Pell pitched the van in a residential area of Kilmarnock and it proved such a hit that it gave him the impetus to open this bricks-and-mortar venue in the town. The brand's signature orange and black colour scheme (which extends to the custom La Marzocco) offers a sunny welcome to those who make the trip to drink great coffee and chinwag with Stuart, his brother Matthew and the rest of the team.

INSIDER'S TIP: CHECK OUT THE RETAIL SHELVES AND PICK UP A BAG OF EK BLEND, GROUND TO YOUR SPECIFICATION

This friendly chatter is fuelled by the Espresso Kart Blend beans, which are crafted in Glasgow by Thomson's. Built into the rustic brew bar is a glass cabinet crammed with cakes, cookies and brownies, so ordering a flat white without indulging in any extras is quite an achievement.

If your stomach is screaming for something more substantial, filled bagels, sourdough sandwiches and loaded salads will hit the spot, but, for serious eats, don't miss the legendary Scottish Burrito. The wrap stuffed with chicken, haggis, chorizo, mozzarella, cheddar, chipotle and garlic mayo delivers big time.

ESTABLISHED
2018

KEY ROASTER
Thomson's
Coffee Roasters

BREWING METHOD
Espresso,
filter,
cold brew

MACHINE
La Marzocco
Linea Classic

GRINDER
Mazzer Kony S

OPENING HOURS
Mon–Sat
8am–3pm
Sun
9am–3pm

 Gluten FREE

 BEANS AVAILABLE INSTORE

 WIFI

 CYCLE FRIENDLY

 OUTDOOR SEATING

 BRING YOUR OWN Cup

 COFFEE COURSES

 DOG FRIENDLY

espressokart.co.uk   07506 444099

 @espressokart @espressokartbar @espressokart

43 KINGS COFFEE & BOOKS

12 Queensberry Street, Dumfries, Dumfries and Galloway, DG1 1EX

This independent bookshop and artisan cafe has weathered the pressures of the high street since 1998, enduring economic highs and lows to provide a welcoming space where the people of Dumfries can gather to enjoy great coffee and company.

The social enterprise (part of a local Christian charity) has such a gleaming reputation in the town and beyond that it was included in *The Independent*'s roundup of top 50 UK coffee shops. A pillar of Kings' success is its top-drawer beans, which the team source from Hasbean and supplement with guest coffees from a range of interesting roasteries.

INSIDER'S TIP CHECK OUT THE SEASONALLY CHANGING PLANT-WALL ART INSTALLATION

On-point caffeine is complemented by an inclusive food offering (there are plenty of plant-based, veggie and gluten-free options) crafted from ultra-fresh local produce. The menu changes seasonally, but visitors can expect to tuck into the likes of toasted sourdough layered with tomato, pesto and mozzarella, and pancakes topped with sticky maple bacon.

The Kings crew are passionate about giving back to the local area and, alongside running community projects, contribute to the regeneration of the town centre.

ESTABLISHED
1998

KEY ROASTER
Hasbean

BREWING METHOD
Espresso, AeroPress, pourover, cold brew

MACHINE
La Marzocco Linea

GRINDER
Nuova Simonelli Mythos One

OPENING HOURS
Mon–Sat 9.30am–5pm

 Gluten FREE

 BEANS AVAILABLE INSTORE

 WIFI

 CYCLE FRIENDLY

 OUTDOOR seating

 DISABLED ACCESS

 BRING YOUR OWN cup

 COFFEE COURSES

 DOG FRIENDLY

kings-online.co.uk   01387 254444

f @kingscoffeeandbooks   🐦 @kingsdumfries   📷 @kingscoffeedumfries

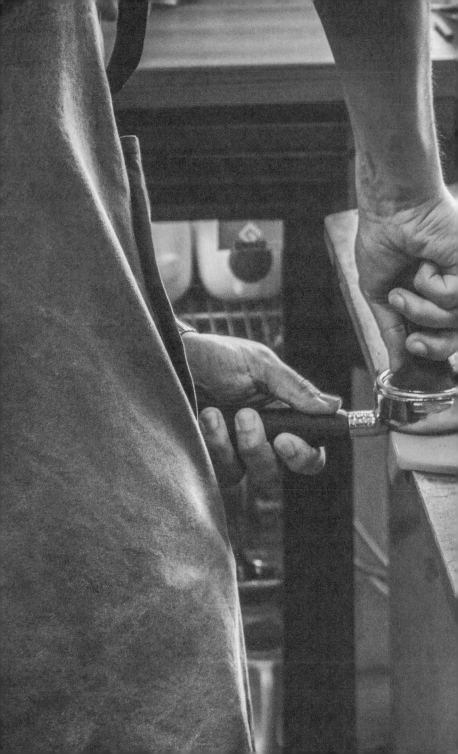

AREA
2
ROASTERIES
AND TRAINER

44 HINBA COFFEE ROASTERS

Balvicar, Isle of Seil, Argyll, Oban

'Pure Air, Pure Taste, Pure Hebridean' is the motto at this west coast roastery which was established to craft top-tier coffee while also preserving the beautiful natural environment in which it is made.

While travelling the world, founders Fergus McCoss and Ness Achilles were so bowled over by the speciality coffee they encountered that when they returned to Scotland in 2019 they set up a roastery on the Isle of Seil. The following year they opened a cafe in Oban (which morphs into a gin bar in the evenings) and chased that with a cafe in Glasgow in 2022.

'FAIRTRADE AND SUSTAINABILITY ARE AS IMPORTANT AS FLAVOUR'

Each season, the pair select single-origin beans from all over the globe and roast them in the unpolluted air of the Hebrides on a Giesen W15A. As well as stocking their own cafes, they sell beans online and on-site. Curious coffee fans can even book an appointment for a tour of the roastery.

Fairtrade and sustainability are as important as flavour for the Hinba team, so they prefer to work with partners who also prioritise the planet.

ESTABLISHED
2019

ROASTER MAKE & SIZE
Giesen W15A
15kg

OPEN
BY APPOINTMENT

BEANS
AVAILABLE

hinba.co.uk   07946 591747
f *@hinba.coffee.roasters* ◎ *@hinba.coffee.roasters*

45 THOMSON'S COFFEE ROASTERS

Burnfield Avenue, Thornliebank, Glasgow, G46 7TL

Thomson's is Scotland's oldest coffee roastery, a proudly independent family business that blends nearly two centuries of coffee heritage with contemporary innovation.

The experienced team tame a trio of powerful roasters (a Whitmee antique flame roaster, a Loring Kestrel and the UK's first Diedrich DR25) to painstakingly preserve the natural flavours of the beans they've sourced. Provenance is a priority and coffees are carefully selected from farms across the coffee-growing belt.

'BLENDING NEARLY TWO CENTURIES OF COFFEE HERITAGE WITH CONTEMPORARY INNOVATION'

Having mastered roasting, Thomson's is now conquering cakes too. Collaborating with local indie Short Long Black, the team have converted part of the roastery warehouse into a bakery. Sample the goods at cafe 1841 on Vinicombe Street, Thomson's HQ (espresso bar, offices and retail showroom) on Fenwick Road and Short Long Black's venue on Victoria Road.

Own-roasted coffee and house-blended teas are available for home delivery and wholesale orders from the Thomson's website, alongside essential brew kit and gifts for coffee lovers.

ESTABLISHED
1841

ROASTER MAKE & SIZE
Diedrich 25kg
Loring Kestrel 35kg
Whitmee 35kg

OPEN
BY APPOINTMENT

BEANS
AVAILABLE

ONLINE

thomsonscoffee.com   **01416 370683**

f @thomsonscoffee   🐦 @thomsonscoffee   📷 @thomsonscoffee

46 FOWER COFFEE

Unit 2a Hamilton Road Industrial Estate, Strathaven, South Lanarkshire, ML10 6UB

In 2020, speciality coffee enthusiast Stuart Jamieson did what so many only dream of doing and left his corporate career to start roasting coffee full-time. Within six months, and with the help of family and friends, he'd converted a former metal factory in Strathaven into his dream roastery.

The result of Stuart's unwavering ambition is a unique roastery cafe that doubles up as a pop-up restaurant and events space. He's created a place where the Fower team can roast top-grade beans and where coffee fans can come together to sample delicious brews.

'OUR GOAL IS TO CREATE MICRO MOMENTS OF JOY'

A key part of Fower's appeal is its down-to-earth ethos: Stuart and co source, roast, grind and brew according to what's in season with the straightforward aim of making great coffee that people will enjoy. The team focus on appreciating the complexities of coffee production without being constrained by them. Stuart explains:

'Our goal is to create micro moments of joy for as many people as we can. These moments shouldn't be bombarded with unnecessary or irrelevant information. There's more to life than a drink although, if we had to pick one, it'd be coffee.'

ESTABLISHED
2021

ROASTER MAKE & SIZE
Diedrich IR-5
5kg

CAFE ONSITE

BEANS AVAILABLE

fowercoffee.com   01357 526241
f @fowercoffee @fowercoffee

47 KAYLA THE COFFEE COACH

31 Elie Road, Blantyre, Glasgow, G72 0GX

ESTABLISHED
2010

COFFEE COURSES

Freelance barista trainer Michaela (Kayla) Jamieson provides pro guidance and practical expertise for both bean novices and not-so-newbies.

Her HQ is the caffeine-rich city of Glasgow, but Kayla travels the UK using her 11 years' experience in the speciality coffee industry to teach baristas of all levels. Whether trainees are total beginners in need of the coffee basics or intermediate-level baristas looking to perfect their brewing abilities, she's got a course or bespoke training programme to fit the bill.

Kayla trains students to impeccably high standards on-site at their own coffee venues. The benefits are that the students feel at ease, while also getting to polish their skills using the equipment they work on day-to-day.

'KAYLA TRAINS STUDENTS TO IMPECCABLY HIGH STANDARDS ON-SITE AT THEIR OWN COFFEE VENUES'

Check out Kayla's Instagram grid to scroll images of just-trained baristas celebrating their coffee accomplishments and see snaps of achieved-at-last latte art. The sea of smiling faces is testament to how she makes the experience as enjoyable as it is informative.

07714 506683
@kaylathecoffeecoach

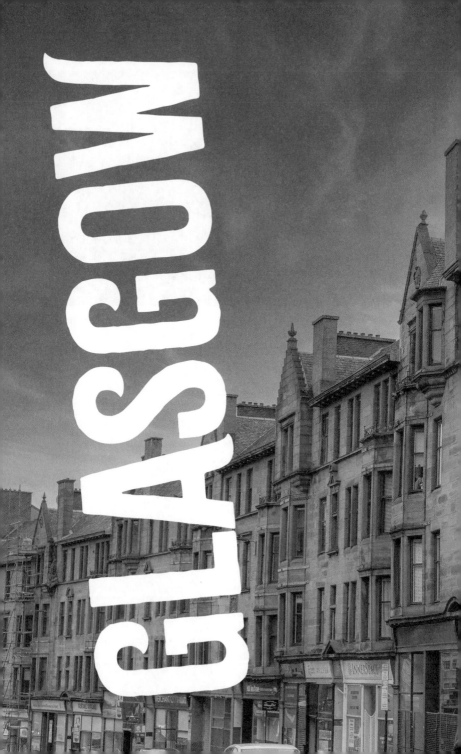

CAFES

ROASTERY

Find more good cafes and roasteries on
pages 132–137

All locations are approximate

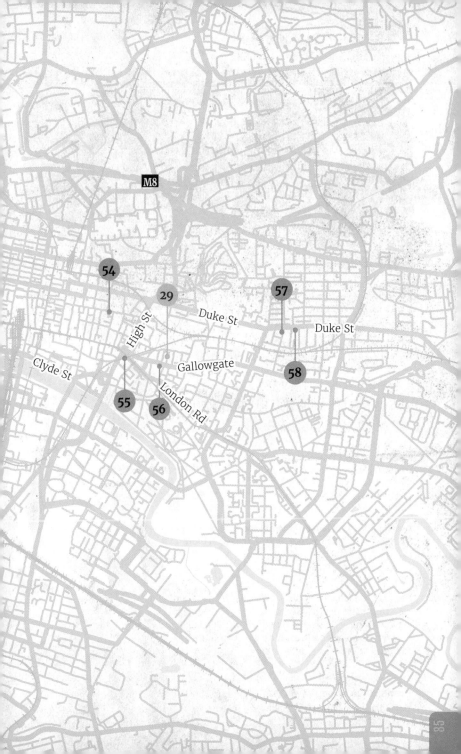

48 HINBA – GLASGOW

86 Dumbarton Road, Glasgow, G11 6NX

Hinba is an old Gaelic word meaning 'isle of the sea', and the moniker of this cool city cafe makes sense when you know that its roastery is located on the beautiful Isle of Seil in Argyll.

Hinba owners Fergus McCoss and Ness Achilles followed the creation of the roastery with a coffee shop in Oban, which was so successful they decided to bring the island vibes to this corner of Glasgow too.

CHECK OUT THE ONLINE STORE FOR A WIDER RANGE OF SPECIALITY BEANS

Purity is the watchword at the ethically driven company. Fergus and Ness travelled the world before returning to their roots, and their passion for coffee quality and flavour is matched only by their commitment to Fairtrade and sustainability.

All of the coffee served here is single origin, seasonally selected and roasted in the pure Hebridean surroundings. Choose from espresso or batch brew prep methods and pair your pick with a pastry or an empanada from the selection of treats – or go large with a proper brunch.

Regulars who enjoy a tipple as much as a coffee should visit Hinba after hours (Wednesdays to Saturdays) to explore the new evening cocktail menu. The team have also recently opened a "real life" shop within the cafe to supplement the online coffee store.

ESTABLISHED
2022

KEY ROASTER
Hinba Coffee Roasters

BREWING METHOD
Espresso, V60

MACHINE
Slayer Steam EP

GRINDER
Compak F8

OPENING HOURS
Mon–Sun
9am–4pm

hinba.co.uk 07944 953547
f @hinba.coffee.roasters @hinba.coffee.roasters

49 1841

14 Vinicombe Street, Glasgow, G12 8BG

Named after the year in which Thomson's Coffee Roasters (Scotland's oldest roastery and the iconic outfit behind this Glasgow gem) was founded, 1841 is a must-visit for the caffeine curious.

A collaboration between Thomson's and a former employee, the cafe is a fantastic opportunity to sip brews crafted from speciality beans direct from the roastery. Those who make the trip can expect a calibre of barista only honed by a company that doesn't compromise in its quest for the exceptional.

WITH BREW KIT, BAKES AND BEANS FOR SALE, YOU PROBABLY WON'T LEAVE EMPTY HANDED

Espresso, filter, hand brew and iced filter coffees are served in a setting created by local artists and craftspeople. The community cafe has been recognised by *Condé Nast Traveller* as one of its *'best coffee shops in Glasgow'*, so locals now rub shoulders with cofficionados from far and wide.

The Thomson's team have recently turned their hands to baking, turning out cakes that are as satisfying as the coffee. Daily deliveries from the Giffnock bakery are accompanied by toasties (made with Freedom Bakery sourdough), Burnfield Bakery pastries and Maple Leaf Bakery cakes.

ESTABLISHED
2020

KEY ROASTER
Thomson's Coffee Roasters

BREWING METHOD
Espresso, filter

MACHINE
Victoria Arduino Eagle One

GRINDER
Mahlkonig E80 Supreme GbW, Mahlkonig E65s GbW, Anfim, Ditting 807 Lab Sweet

OPENING HOURS
Mon–Sat
9am–5pm
Sun
10am–5pm

 Gluten FREE

 BEANS AVAILABLE INSTORE

 WIFI

 CYCLE FRIENDLY

 OUTDOOR SEATING

 DISABLED ACCESS

 BRING YOUR OWN Cup.

 DOG FRIENDLY

1841.coffee   07734 939514
f @1841.coffee   @1841.coffee

50 PERCH & REST

39 Otago Street, Glasgow, G12 8JJ

This family-run coffee shop in Glasgow's West End is near the university, so its alfresco tables and countertop cabinet of freshly baked cakes and pastries lure students craving a caffeinated pick-me-up between lectures.

A bright and airy Aladdin's cave of speciality coffee delights, it's packed with all manner of kit to help visitors recreate the magic at home. Visitors can pick up brewers, drippers, grinders, scales and, of course, an assortment of top-notch beans to experiment with.

WHEN THE TEMPERATURE SOARS, ORDER A SMOOTH AND CREAMY NITRO COLD BREW

Especially covetable among all this gear is the cafe's own sleek Curtis Seraphim brewer. It's the only one of its kind in Scotland and delivers consistently top-notch V60 single serves. Experience it for yourself as you try guest coffees from European roasteries such as Kafferäven, Sumo, Kawa and Nomad, or plump for an espresso-based drink made with house beans roasted by Gardelli.

ESTABLISHED
2019

KEY ROASTER
Gardelli Speciality Coffees

BREWING METHOD
Espresso, V60, nitro

MACHINE
Slayer Steam X

GRINDER
Mahlkonig EK43, Compak PKF DBW, Mahlkonig K30 Air

OPENING HOURS
Mon-Fri
8.30am-6pm
Sat 9am-6pm
Sun 10am-5pm

 Gluten FREE

 BEANS AVAILABLE INSTORE

 CYCLE FRIENDLY

 OUTDOOR SEATING

 DISABLED ACCESS

 BRING YOUR OWN Cup.

 DOG FRIENDLY

prestcoffee.com   **01413 410229**
f @perchandrest   @ @perchandrest

51 OTTOMAN COFFEEHOUSE

73 Berkeley Street, Glasgow, G3 7DX

Stepping inside Ottoman Coffeehouse is an absolute feast for the senses. Evoking the aesthetic, grandeur and bustling atmosphere of the historic coffee houses of Istanbul, this is a place to unshackle yourself from your regular coffee order and be immersed in an unusual sensory experience.

Ask for an Ottoman Coffee Brew crafted with finely ground, lightly roasted beans and brewed Turkish-style in a copper ibrik (the world's oldest coffee brewing method). Or order a single origin via syphon and watch as the Wonka-esque contraption produces whistle-clean, full-bodied filter coffee.

 INSIDER'S TIP — FOR OUTRAGEOUS INDULGENCE, ORDER THE DECADENT RED VELVET LATTE

Rather than hassle and harry customers in order to free up tables, the team at this popular spot encourage visitors to take their time and lounge in the ever-so-comfy sofas while sampling delights from the vast coffee list.

Want more time to soak up the salubrious surroundings? There's also a Middle Eastern-inspired food menu which features deliciously authentic street-food dishes such as kebabs and shawarma salads.

ESTABLISHED
2015

KEY ROASTER
Multiple roasteries

BREWING METHOD
Espresso, cafetiere, Chemex, ibrik, Japanese cold drip, syphon, V60

MACHINE
Faema E61, Faema E71

GRINDER
Compak PK100, Mahlkonig EK43 T, Mythos One, Mythos 2

OPENING HOURS
Tue-Sat
8am-7pm
Sun 9am-7pm

 Gluten FREE

 BEANS AVAILABLE — INSTORE

 WIFI

 CYCLE FRIENDLY

 BRING YOUR OWN Cup

ottomancoffeehouse.co.uk   01415 885982
f @ottomancoffeehouse @ottomancoffeehouse

52 WILLOW GROVE

531 Sauchiehall Street, Glasgow, G3 7PQ

After living in Melbourne, Willow Grove founder Adele McPhee was inspired to recreate a slice of antipodean coffee culture in her home town of Glasgow.

Her vision proved exceptionally popular and, on weekday mornings, there's almost always a queue of commuters lining the electric-blue exterior awaiting their pre-work fix. Weekends are just as busy and tables within are chock-full of locals tucking into drool-inducing brunch and lunch dishes.

 INSIDER'S TIP CAN'T CHOOSE FROM THE BRUNCH LINE-UP? MAKE LIKE A LOCAL AND ORDER THE CHORIZO SHAKSHUKA

Adele usually has four different brewing methods on the go at any one time, so there's plenty to try if you want to switch up your usual flat white. Guest coffees are updated monthly, but don't fret if you fall in love with one in particular as the most popular roasteries (such as Stirling's Unorthodox, Missing Bean in Oxford, France's Moklair and Fidela in Northern Ireland) make regular reappearances.

Sauchiehall Street venue packed out? Try nearby sister site, Willow Grove Edington, inside the Scottish Opera Production Studios (closed on weekends).

ESTABLISHED
2017

KEY ROASTER
The Gatehouse Coffee Roasters

BREWING METHOD
Espresso, V60, batch brew, Chemex

MACHINE
Rancilio

GRINDER
Eureka Helios 80, Fiorenzato F83, Fiorenzato F5G

OPENING HOURS
Mon–Fri
8.30am–4.30pm
Sat
9am–4pm

 Gluten FREE

 BEANS AVAILABLE INSTORE

 WIFI

 CYCLE FRIENDLY

 OUTDOOR SEATING

 DISABLED ACCESS

 BRING YOUR OWN Cup

 DOG FRIENDLY

willowgrovecoffee.com   01412 373490
f @willowgrovecoffee   @ @willowgrovecoffee

53 SPRIGG

264 Sauchiehall Street, Glasgow, G2 3EQ

C raving a nutritional boost after perusing the stores on Glasgow's busy Sauchiehall Street? Make a beeline for this contemporary lunch stop where you can pick up a takeaway container stuffed with a kaleidoscopic array of fresh veggies.

This Sauchiehall site is the big sister venue of the original Sprigg in Merchant City, which has long been a favourite with office folk looking for a more inspiring lunch than a supermarket meal deal.

 INSIDER'S TIP **BEAT THE QUEUES: DOWNLOAD THE NEW SPRIGG APP FOR EFFORTLESS PRE-ORDERING**

Reassuringly, the coffee line-up at both establishments is as inventive as the salads. The house blend comes from Glasgow's The Good Coffee Cartel, and there's also a regular rotation of guest filters from Scottish favourites such as Thomson's, Glen Lyon and Dear Green. In summer, ready-to-go cold brew from Two Birds and Minor Figures are available, as well as Kombucha from Living Tea which is brewed in the city.

Fancy a Sprigg at home? You can now order your favourite food bowl on Deliveroo.

ESTABLISHED
2018

KEY ROASTER
The Good
Coffee Cartel

BREWING METHOD
Espresso, filter

MACHINE
Kees van der
Westen Mirage

GRINDER
Mythos One,
Mahlkonig EK43

OPENING HOURS
Mon–Fri
8am–3pm
Sat
11am–3pm

 Gluten FREE

 BEANS AVAILABLE INSTORE

 WIFI

 CYCLE FRIENDLY

 OUTDOOR seating

 DISABLED ACCESS

 BRING YOUR OWN Cup

 DOG FRIENDLY

sprigg.co.uk   **07483 106438**
f @wearesprigg   @wearesprigg

54 SPITFIRE ESPRESSO

127 Candleriggs, Merchant City, Glasgow, G1 1NP

A pillar of Glasgow's speciality scene since 2015, Spitfire is loved by locals for its consistently on-point espresso, banging breakfast burritos and life's-too-short-not-to-have-fun vibe.

Founder Danny Gorton's trusty house blend, Gunnerbeans, is roasted across the city by the pros at Thomson's and is a bespoke mix of Colombian and Brazilian beans. There are guest options too (all available as espresso, batch and cold brew) from Jericho, Dark Arts and Roundhill.

 THREE NEW SISTER SITES HAVE POPPED UP IN OFFICE SPACES ACROSS THE CITY – CHECK SOCIAL FOR DEETS

Danny and team adopt the same local and sustainable sourcing ethos when it comes to the food menu, using ingredients from the likes of Pennyfield Eggs in Kilmarnock, Puddledub Pork in Auchtertool and FacePlant Foods in Edinburgh. Sample them in all-day breakfast dishes such as the poached eggs and smoked salmon bagel, and the full Scottish.

Grab a stool by the window to watch the Merchant City action or plonk yourself on a banquette at the back of the high-ceilinged space to lose yourself in a book.

ESTABLISHED
2015

KEY ROASTER
Thomson's Coffee Roasters

BREWING METHOD
Espresso, batch brew, cold brew

MACHINE
La Marzocco FB70

GRINDER
Mythos One

OPENING HOURS
Fri–Sat 8am–6pm
Sun–Thu 8am–5pm

spitfireespresso.com   **07578 250105**
f @spitfireespresso @ @spitfireglasgow

55 OUTLIER

38 London Road, Glasgow, G1 5NB

As if this industrial-style cafe in a former glass factory wasn't cool enough, in summer 2023 it will be bolstered by a wine bar, dining garden and art gallery. Until then, visit to enjoy a cardamom and custard bun or a slice of butterscotch and rye banana bread and an expertly crafted brew.

Award-winning head of coffee Tony Lee Johnson roasts all of the beans himself, providing the goods for filter, batch, espresso and AeroPress brew methods. Those who find themselves hooked on the house blend can also pick up a bag for home brewing.

 OUTLIER IS BUILT ON SUSTAINABILITY AND ALSO SUPPORTS LOCAL FOOD BANKS

Outlier has recently found itself included in *Condé Nast Traveller*'s Best Restaurants in Glasgow list, which makes sense when you know that most of the edibles are crafted at the on-site bakery. Breads are 100 per cent sourdough while cakes and pastries deliver maximum flavour. As the goods are rustled up in an open-plan kitchen, visitors can witness the work that goes into their carby creations while chowing down on a legendary fried chicken ciabatta with hot honey XO sauce.

ESTABLISHED
2022

KEY ROASTER
The Good Coffee Cartel

BREWING METHOD
Espresso, filter, batch brew, AeroPress

MACHINE
Kees van der Westen Spirit Duette

GRINDER
Anfim SP II, Mahlkonig EK43 S

OPENING HOURS
Tue-Fri
8am-4pm
Sat
8am-5pm
Sun
9am-5pm

 Gluten FREE

 BEANS AVAILABLE INSTORE

 OUTDOOR Seating

 DISABLED ACCESS

 BRING YOUR OWN Cup

 DOG FRIENDLY

 f @outlier-coffee-bakery @outlier.gla

DEAR GREEN®

ONLINE SHOP
WHOLESALE COFFEE
SCA TRAINING
B CORP CERTIFIED

Certified

(B)

Corporation

This company meets the
highest standards of social
and environmental impact

Living
Wage
Foundation

1% FOR THE PLANET

56 US V THEM

200 Gallowgate, Glasgow, G1 5DR

Any good barista in Glasgow has Us V Them on speed dial for those mornings when their espresso machine doesn't want to play ball. Founded by James Aitken in 2017, the sales, installation and servicing company is the go-to for coffee kit repairs across the city and beyond.

With all that expert knowledge at his fingertips, it was only a matter of time before James went native and opened his own coffee bar. By looking to cafes in Brooklyn and Los Angeles for inspiration, he's crafted a venue unlike anything else in Scotland: steel columns, chequered flooring and a striking black communal table create a unique industrial-minimalist vibe.

 CHECK OUT THE CHILLED DRINK SPECIALS – THE COLD BREW TONIC IS A SUMMER WINNER

However great the aesthetics, the focus is very much on coffee. The main roaster changes each quarter and is usually a Scottish supplier such as James' former colleagues at Dear Green. Beans from Europe and further afield take turns on the guest grinders – Barcelona's Three Marks Coffee recently featured.

The space also houses James' workshop, so visitors can watch the engineer servicing espresso machines as they sip shots pulled through a slick white Slayer Steam. James is an SCA-authorised trainer too and relishes passing on his learning to each new league of coffee technicians.

ESTABLISHED
2020

KEY ROASTER
Multiple
roasteries

BREWING METHOD
Espresso,
batch brew

MACHINE
Slayer Steam LP

GRINDER
Mazzer Kold,
Mahlkonig
EK43,
Mahlkonig E65s
GbW, Mazzer
Super Jolly V Pro

OPENING HOURS
Tue-Sun
9am-4pm

 Gluten FREE

 BEANS AVAILABLE INSTORE

 WIFI

 CYCLE FRIENDLY

 OUTDOOR seating

 DISABLED ACCESS

 BRING YOUR OWN Cup

 COFFEE COURSES

DOG FRIENDLY

usvthem.coffee   07734 888365
 @usvthemcoffee

57 MAYZE

172 Sword Street, Dennistoun, Glasgow, G31 1SE

Mayze might be a newcomer in Dennistoun but, thanks to its flagship cafe in Finnieston, this fresher is already enjoying a quality reputation on the Glasgow coffee scene.

The original venue is famed for its revolving bean selection and the options at this new site are just as varied. The bill of beans from European roasteries changes weekly so each visit delivers a deliciously unique brew experience. Whether you're sipping a peachy Girls Who Grind coffee on batch or indulging in chocolatey Cairngorm beans pulled as espresso, novelty comes as standard.

 SPECIAL OCCASION COMING UP? PRE-ORDER A MAYZE CELEBRATION CAKE

The focus on quality and creativity continues in the Mayze kitchen, where the team rustle up a seasonal menu of veggie eats. No time to stick around for brekkie or lunch? Nab one of the gargantuan homemade pastries or plant-based sosij rolls to take away.

There are big things planned at this little cafe in 2023, including the launch of a wholesale and catering arm. Watch this space.

ESTABLISHED
2022

KEY ROASTER
Multiple roasteries

BREWING METHOD
Espresso, batch brew

MACHINE
Astoria Storm

GRINDER
Compak GTW

OPENING HOURS
Mon–Fri
8.30am–4pm
Sat
9am–5pm
Sun
10am–4pm

 Gluten FREE

 BEANS AVAILABLE / INSTORE

 WIFI

 CYCLE FRIENDLY

 OUTDOOR SEATING

 DISABLED ACCESS

 BRING YOUR OWN CUP

 DOG FRIENDLY

mayze.co.uk
f @mayze_dennistoun @mayze_dennistoun

58 ZENNOR

354 Duke Street, Glasgow, G31 1RB

Glasgow's East End has long been a mecca for young people and creatives thanks to its slew of independent pubs and eateries. If the west of the city is the gentrified big sister, the east has an edgier, younger-sibling vibe.

So, with its sleek minimalist interior and curated selection of speciality beans, new East End coffee shop Zennor fits right in.

The Zennor team roast their coffee in-house, sourcing green beans from around the world. What's available as espresso, batch, hand and cold brew changes seasonally. However, you can be assured that whatever you choose will be expertly crafted by the clued-up baristas. If you like what you're served in the cafe, you can buy a bag of beans in-store (or online) to brew at home.

 ZENNOR IS SUPER DOG FRIENDLY SO FEEL FREE TO MOOCH WITH YOUR POOCH

Fortifying the own-roasted goods is a rotation of guest coffees from hero roasteries such as Origin, Obadiah, Campbell and Syme, and New Ground. Take your pick from the ever-changing selection and curl up on one of the comfy lounge chairs with a brew, a slice of homemade carrot cake and a good book. Don't worry about dropping by without any reading material as the cafe stocks a stack of indie books and magazines – *Sip 'n' Slurp* by Freda Yuan is the baristas' fave.

ESTABLISHED
2021

KEY ROASTER
Zennor

BREWING METHOD
Espresso,
batch brew,
cold brew,
hand brew

MACHINE
La Marzocco
KB90

GRINDER
Mahlkonig
EK43,
Mahlkonig E65S
GbW, Mythos
One

OPENING HOURS
Mon-Fri
8am-5pm
Sat-Sun
9am-5pm

 Gluten FREE

 BEANS AVAILABLE INSTORE

 WIFI

 BRING YOUR OWN Cup.

 COFFEE COURSES

 DOG FRIENDLY

zennorcoffee.co.uk
@zennor.glasgow

59 THE GOOD COFFEE CARTEL

12 Cornwall Street, Glasgow, G41 1AQ

B uilt on the mantra of 'We want to do good', this roastery cafe is on a mission to make incredible coffee as sustainable as possible.

The original "tin-fluencers", The Good Coffee Cartel team are pioneers of the green movement within the Scottish coffee scene thanks to their reusable packaging (own-roasted beans are sold in refillable tins). It was also one of the first coffee shops in the city to offer a cup exchange: for a small deposit, customers who have forgotten their reusable cup can borrow one when ordering to-go.

 SUCKER FOR A FLAT WHITE? TRY A MILKY BOI

Doing good extends to the team's approach to sourcing greens for the house roasts: they only partner with suppliers who actively ensure sustainability for farmers. The coffee offering rotates regularly, so there's always a full selection of flavours on offer and beans range from comfy *'coffees that taste like coffee'* to weird and wonderful releases.

A recent refurb has introduced a new bar and seating area in which coffee fans can sample the latest blends and single origins and chow down on one of the city's famous Doh doughnuts.

ESTABLISHED
2017

KEY ROASTER
The Good Coffee Cartel

BREWING METHOD
Espresso, Orea, AeroPress, Kalita Wave, batch brew

MACHINE
Kees Van Der Westen Spirit

GRINDER
Mahlkonig EK43, Anfim SCODY II, Mythos One

OPENING HOURS
Mon–Sun
9am–4pm

thegoodcoffeecartel.com 07738 277983

@thegoodcoffeecartel

GLASGOW ROASTERY

60 DEAR GREEN COFFEE ROASTERS

Unit 2, 13-27 East Campbell Street, Glasgow, G1 5DT

Dear Green is one of Scotland's foremost roasteries and the first to earn B Corp status. The team are truly committed to putting the planet before profit.

Not only is Dear Green on a path to net zero – having ditched single-use plastics for reusable coffee buckets and recyclable packaging – it also displays a determined social conscience. A recent collab with the charity Social Bite resulted in £1 from every bag of coffee sold going to help end homelessness in Scotland.

'THE TEAM ARE TRULY COMMITTED TO PUTTING THE PLANET BEFORE PROFIT'

Founder Lisa Lawson has also built lasting partnerships in other parts of the world, including with coffee producers such as the Rama Women's Association in Burundi, the AMACA group of female producers in Colombia, and the Tumba, Bombe and Odaco washing stations in Rwanda and Ethiopia. Her aim is always to source beans as ethically as possible.

Earlier this year, Lisa and crew signed up to the World Coffee Research Checkoff Program where, for every kilo of coffee bought, a donation is made to help grow, protect and enhance coffee supplies and improve the livelihoods of the families who produce it.

ESTABLISHED
2011

ROASTER MAKE & SIZE
Probat P5 5kg
Probat P25 25kg
Probat L12 12kg

OPEN
BY APPOINTMENT

COFFEE
COURSES

COURSES

BEANS
AVAILABLE

deargreencoffee.com   01415 527774
f @deargreencoffeeroastersglasgow 🐦 @coffeeglasgow ⊙ @deargreen

AREA

3

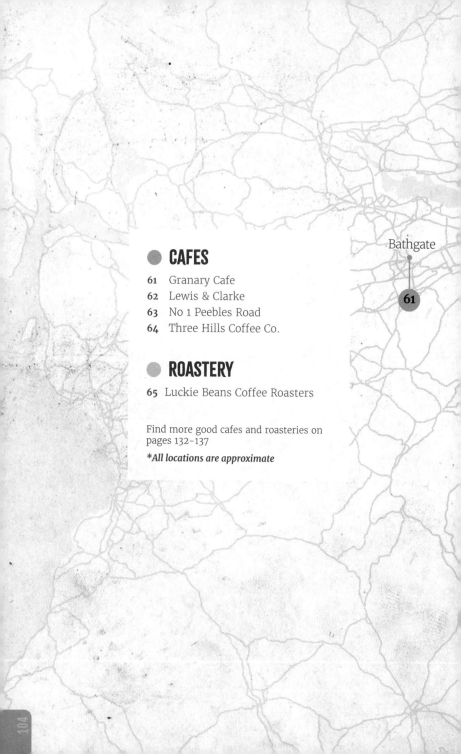

● CAFES

● ROASTERY

Find more good cafes and roasteries on pages 132–137

All locations are approximate

Bathgate

61

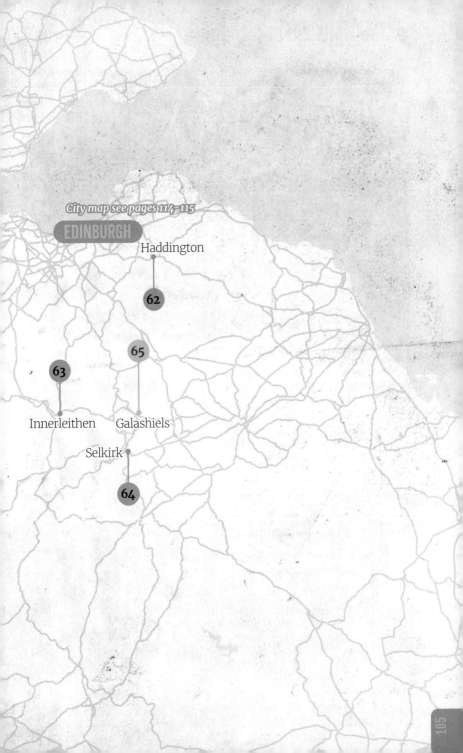

City map see pages 114–115

EDINBURGH

Haddington

62

65

63

Innerleithen   Galashiels

Selkirk

64

61 GRANARY CAFE

37 North Bridge Street, Bathgate, West Lothian, EH48 4PL

Linlithgow's Granary Cafe has garnered a glowing reputation for its quality food and drink over the years, so expectations were high when, in 2022, the team opened this takeout sister venue in Bathgate.

It was the success of selling cafe food to-go during lockdown that gave Granary founder David Stein the confidence to take the plunge and open a second site. Happily, the takeaway coffee and food concept has been a hit, and locals and holidaymakers queue to get their hands on freshly roasted beans from Glen Lyon in Aberfeldy.

 START THE DAY WITH ONE OF GRANARY'S ARTISAN BREAKFAST ROLLS OR A STUFFED CROISSANT

A crew of talented chefs and daily deliveries of uber-fresh ingredients ensure there's always an exciting menu of edibles to accompany the coffee. Creations for carnivores (such as the smoked bacon, avo, chilli, lime and mature cheddar toastie) feature meat from David's own butcher shop, while toothsome traybakes, light-as-a-feather scones and on-point pastries arrive each morning from the sister bakery.

ESTABLISHED
2022

KEY ROASTER
Glen Lyon
Coffee Roasters

BREWING METHOD
Espresso

MACHINE
Esprezzi

GRINDER
Fiorenzato F64E

OPENING HOURS
Mon–Fri
8am–4pm
Sat–Sun
9am–4pm

 Gluten FREE

 BEANS AVAILABLE INSTORE

 WIFI

 BRING YOUR OWN Cup

 DOG FRIENDLY

granary.scot
f @granarybathgate @thegranarybathgate

62 LEWIS & CLARKE

2a Main Street, Gifford, Haddington, East Lothian, EH41 4QH

Lewis & Clarke offers the kind of cafe experience you'd expect in the heart of Edinburgh or Glasgow rather than a quiet East Lothian village. Solid oak furniture, restaurant-level crockery and tables bathed in natural light give the coffee shop an air of casual refinement.

The food and drink is as pleasing as the surroundings thanks to a secret weapon: the talent of co-owner and pastry chef Kate Lewis, who cut her teeth at some of the country's top Michelin-rated restaurants. Sample her delectable work in an afternoon tea of homemade sausage rolls, mini toasted sandwiches, scones and cakes.

 INSIDER'S TIP **LOCALS FLOCK FOR THE REGULAR POP-UP DINNERS AND SUNDAY LUNCHES – CHECK SOCIAL FOR DETAILS**

The accompanying speciality coffee travels south from Glen Lyon Coffee Roasters in the Highlands and is available as espresso or pourover via Moccamaster. Quality coffee is bolstered by a solid line-up of loose-leaf teas and hot chocolates.

In summer, grab a table outside and watch the world go by as you indulge in a brew and a Cherry Kiss – Lewis & Clarke's delicious take on a classic black forest gateau.

ESTABLISHED
2018

KEY ROASTER
Glen Lyon
Coffee Roasters

BREWING METHOD
Espresso,
Moccamaster,
cold brew

MACHINE
Futurmat Ariete
F3

GRINDER
Zenith 65 E HS

OPENING HOURS
Wed–Sun
10am–4pm
(seasonal opening hours)

 Gluten FREE

 BEANS AVAILABLE / INSTORE

 WIFI

 CYCLE FRIENDLY

 OUTDOOR SEATING

 DISABLED ACCESS

 BRING YOUR OWN CUP

 DOG FRIENDLY

lcartisan.co.uk   01620 811001

f @lewisandclarkeartisankitchen   🐦 @lcartisan   📷 @lcartisan

63 NO 1 PEEBLES ROAD

1 Peebles Road, Innerleithen, Scottish Borders, EH44 6QX

Be prepared to cosy up next to mountain bikers, hikers and outdoor adventurers at this uber-popular coffee shop in the shadows of the Elibank and Traquair Forest. Whatever time of year you drop by, sharing tables and getting to know the other punters is a fun and unavoidable part of the No 1 Peebles Road experience.

The constant stream of visitors is a result of founders Emma Perry and Craig Anderson meeting their straightforward objective: *'to serve braw coffee and braw food'*. They achieve this with the help of the roasters at Steampunk Coffee, whose North Berwick beans are transformed into silky espresso (try the house serve Muckle Milky) and pourover filters.

 NO 1'S CAKE CABINET IS CRAMMED WITH HOMEMADE BAKES SUCH AS LEMON POLENTA AND STICKY GINGER

On the food front, sourcing ingredients from local producers and making everything from scratch ensures the edibles are as good as the brews. Fuel a day on the trails with a bulging breakfast burrito or belgian waffles stacked with banana, berries and maple syrup.

ESTABLISHED
2014

KEY ROASTER
Steampunk
Coffee

BREWING METHOD
Espresso,
pourover

MACHINE
La Marzocco
Linea

GRINDER
Eureka Helios
80

OPENING HOURS
Thu–Mon
8am–4.30pm

 Gluten FREE

 BEANS AVAILABLE / INSTORE

 WIFI

 CYCLE FRIENDLY

 OUTDOOR SEATING

 DISABLED ACCESS

 BRING YOUR OWN CUP

 DOG FRIENDLY

no1peeblesroad.coffee   01896 209486
f @no1peeblesroad @no1_peebles_road

64 THREE HILLS COFFEE CO.

23 High Street, Selkirk, TD7 4BZ

No roadtrip along the Scottish Borders is complete without a pit stop at Three Hills Coffee in Selkirk.

Bang in the middle of the town's High Street, the bright and buzzy little cafe has everything you could possibly want from a coffee shop: comfy seating, a friendly-yet-chilled vibe and an above-par choice of roasted-in-house coffee beans.

Named after the triple summits of the nearby Eildons, Three Hills was established as a coffee roastery by Richard Keeling and Jessica Jericevich in 2016. As a result of roaring wholesale trade, the pair took the plunge and opened the cafe in 2018. It was an immediate triumph with locals and visitors looking for a speciality hit, and there are now plans afoot to open a barista training academy in early 2023.

 INSIDER'S TIP OVER CAFFEINATED? TRY A CUP OF THE OWN-ROASTED NUTTY BRAZILIAN DECAF

The beans roasted by the Three Hills team are ethically sourced from farms in Brazil, Colombia, Guatemala and Indonesia. We recommend sampling the house espresso blend Eildon as an americano to savour its bold fruity notes and rich undercurrent of roasted almond and dark chocolate.

ESTABLISHED
2018

KEY ROASTER
Three Hills Coffee

BREWING METHOD
Espresso, drip

MACHINE
Sanremo Café Racer Renegade

GRINDER
Mazzer Major, Mazzer Mini, Mahlkonig E65s GbW

OPENING HOURS
Tue–Fri
9am–4pm
Sat
9.30am–4pm

 Gluten FREE

 BEANS AVAILABLE INSTORE

 OUTDOOR seating

 DISABLED ACCESS

 BRING YOUR OWN Cup

 COFFEE COURSES

 DOG FRIENDLY

threehillscoffee.com   **01750 22322**
f @threehillscoffee   🐦 @3hillscoffee   📷 @threehillscoffee

AREA
3
ROASTERY

65 LUCKIE BEANS COFFEE ROASTERS

38a Bank Street, Galashiels, Scottish Borders, TD1 1EP

Having purchased new premises at the tail end of 2020, Luckie Beans founder Jamie McLuckie spent the best part of 2021 renovating the new roastery in the centre of Galashiels.

At the new HQ, Jamie sources beans via trusted merchants and roasts them on a 15kg Giesen. The ever-popular pick of the bunch is the Love Lane House Blend, which combines beans from Brazil, Guatemala, India and Kenya.

From the single-origin selection, kudos must be paid to the Rwanda Dukunde Kawa Musasa, winner of a two-star Great Taste award in 2022. It was described by judges as having '*a sweet yet light strawberries and cream, Campino confectionery note. Light and fragrant, deliciously elegant. With milk we get a twist of strawberry laces. Refreshing on the palate and delicious.*'

ESTABLISHED
2015

ROASTER MAKE & SIZE
Giesen W15A
15kg

'KUDOS MUST BE PAID TO THE RWANDA DUKUNDE KAWA MUSASA – WINNER OF A TWO-STAR GREAT TASTE AWARD'

As well as supplying speciality shops and cafes across the UK, Luckie Beans delivers its award-winning beans to coffee fans via its online shop and subscription service.

If you're in the area on a Wednesday, you can pop into the roastery shop to pick up a takeaway coffee or a bag of beans to brew at home. Check Instagram for up-to-date opening times.

luckiebeans.co.uk   07810 446537
f @luckiebeans 🐦 @luckie_beans 📷 @luckie_beans

TRINITY

Ferry Rd

B900

73

Duke St

B901

75

Royal Botanic
Garden

Leith Walk

BONNINGTON

B900

STOCKBRIDGE

London Rd

Easter Rd

66

67

69

Dean Village

Palace of Holyro

Edinburgh Castle

70

Queen's Dr

71

68

West Port

A700

Gilmore Pl

Bruntsfield Pl

MARCHMONT

72

MERCHISTON

Colinton Rd

MORNINGSIDE

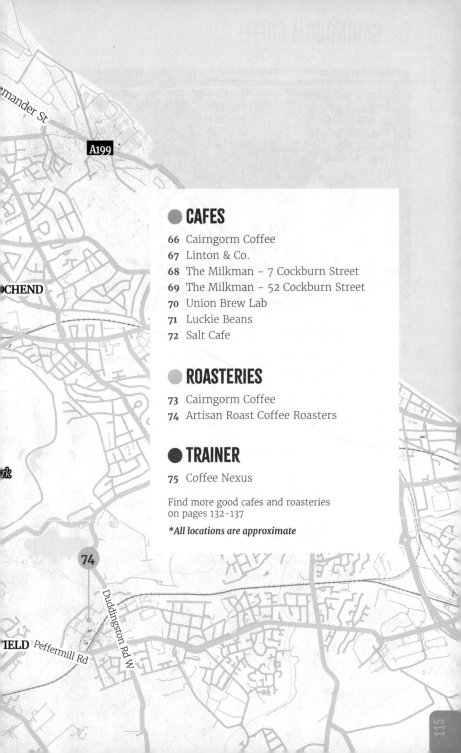

● CAFES

● ROASTERIES

● TRAINER

Find more good cafes and roasteries
on pages 132–137

All locations are approximate

66 CAIRNGORM COFFEE

41a Frederick Street, Edinburgh, EH2 1EP

This tiny coffee bar on Frederick Street is where the Cairngorm story began in 2014. The narrative has progressed to include a larger sister cafe on Melville Place and a roastery in Leith, but this original site is still a favourite with Cairngorm fans who gather to sample exciting coffees prepared by skilled baristas.

The venue offers opportunities to get lost in a Wonka-esque world of flavour. There's an extensive collection of own-roasted beans to choose from, as well as guest options from the likes of Berlin's Five Elephant and Belfast's Lucid Coffee Roasters.

What makes Cairngorm different from any other multi-roastery cafe is its use of the freezer. After roasting, each batch is left to rest for an optimum number of days before being pre-dosed and plunged to sub-zero temperatures to lock in every ounce of flavour.

 DON'T KNOW WHAT TO SAMPLE? ASK THE BARISTAS FOR THEIR PICK OF THE WEEK'S THREE ESPRESSOS

Founder Robi Lambie says: '*Following the pandemic, we have a renewed focus on presenting coffee in the best way possible and on creating an experience for the customer. We want them to be able to enjoy coffee in the same way they might enjoy wine in a wine bar.*'

ESTABLISHED
2014

KEY ROASTER
Cairngorm Coffee

BREWING METHOD
Espresso, V60

MACHINE
Victoria Arduino Eagle One

GRINDER
Mahlkonig EK43

OPENING HOURS
Wed–Sun
9am–5pm

 BEANS AVAILABLE INSTORE

 WIFI

 OUTDOOR seating

 BRING YOUR OWN Cup

COFFEE COURSES

 DOG FRIENDLY

cairngorm.coffee

f @cairngormcoffee 🐦 @cairngormcoffee 📷 @cairngormcoffeeco

67 LINTON & CO.

Unit P3 Waverley Mall Rooftop, Princes Street, Edinburgh, EH1 1BQ

Flanked on all sides by ubiquitous coffee-shop chains, Linton & Co. had to work hard to carve out a niche on the busiest street in the city. Fortunately, owners Alex and Lara had already honed their coffee confidence by slinging shots in their converted vintage Citroën coffee van and relished the opportunity to disrupt the city-centre's status quo.

Within months, they'd etched their place on Edinburgh's speciality coffee scene and established a reputation for great brews (made with beans roasted by Hasbean and Clifton) and baked goods. Menus at the venue are stacked with breakfast and lunch goodies, alongside the famed Linton & Co. brownies.

 CHECK OUT THE WEBSITE FOR HOMEWARES AND BREWING EQUIPMENT

The pair's vintage van (Bernard to friends) now serves coffee from their new cafe and bar at The Hub's terrace on Castlehill. Its expanded offering includes cocktails, craft beers, Italian ice cream (in summer) and warming winter drinks.

ESTABLISHED
2015

KEY ROASTER
Hasbean

BREWING METHOD
Espresso,
batch brew

MACHINE
La Marzocco
Linea Classic

GRINDER
Mahlkonig EK43
Mahlkonig E65s
GbW,

OPENING HOURS
Mon-Fri
8am-5pm
Sat 9am-5pm
Sun 10am-5pm

 BEANS AVAILABLE / INSTORE

 WIFI

 CYCLE FRIENDLY

 OUTDOOR SEATING

 DISABLED ACCESS

 BRING YOUR OWN CUP

lintonandco.com   07525 655587
@Linton & Co.   @linton_and_co

I'm hot.

And here's why.

I'm made from plants, lined with plants and dressed up in water-based ink. Really, the difference between me and a plastic cup is black and white. I'll break down into carbon dioxide, water, and organic matter when in a commercial compost. Now that's a pattern worth repeating.

**Hot Cups that are here for
a good time, not a long time.**

LEARN MORE

decentpackaging.co.uk
@decentpackaging

68 THE MILKMAN – 7 COCKBURN STREET

7 Cockburn Street, Edinburgh, EH1 1BP

This little coffee shop near the Royal Mile should be on any itinerary of Edinburgh must-dos, alongside the ubiquitous tour of the castle and downing a whisky in a Grassmarket pub. Swing by to break up a day of sightseeing with a fortifying coffee (care of Cornish roastery Origin) and consider another highlight ticked off.

Small is beautiful at The Milkman: the premises are tiny but handsome, and the coffee list restrained (just espresso-based drinks and batch brew) but skilfully executed. The team keep the offering modest so they can focus on serving high-quality drinks without the distractions of a large food menu. It works, and sitting at a window seat, sipping a finely foamed flat white while crunching into a buttery pastry and gazing over the looming ancient buildings is utterly charming.

INSIDER'S TIP MILKMAN COLLABS RANGE FROM COFFEE SOAP TO CARDS PAINTED USING OLD COFFEE GROUNDS

Switch up the experience by ordering one of the vegan cinnamon buns, blueberry knots or chocolate babkas and a whistle-clean batch made with beans from the likes of Manifesto, Girls Who Grind, Curve and Fireheart.

The Milkman also has a sister cafe – find it up the road at 52 Cockburn Street.

ESTABLISHED
2015

KEY ROASTER
Origin Coffee Roasters

BREWING METHOD
Espresso, batch brew

MACHINE
La Marzocco Strada AV

GRINDER
Mahlkonig EK43 S, Mythos One

OPENING HOURS
Mon–Sat
8am–5pm
Sun
9am–5pm

themilkman.coffee   **01314 661346**

f @themilkmancoffee   @themilkmanedin   @themilkmancoffee

69 THE MILKMAN – 52 COCKBURN STREET

52 Cockburn Street, Edinburgh, EH1 1PB

Find yourself on attractive Cockburn Street in the heart of Edinburgh and you'll have two opportunities to sample exceptional speciality drinks, care of The Milkman's duo of coffee shops.

The two venues – based at numbers 7 and 52 – each have their own unique vibe but both are reliable for on-point espresso drinks, as well as chai, turmeric and matcha lattes (the key ingredient being supplied by a Japanese matchaeologist). The original (number 7) is your go-to for batch brew, while this newer coffee shop offers pourovers via V60.

INSIDER'S TIP
THE MILKMAN RECENTLY BECAME A LIVING WAGE EMPLOYER

Located just off the Royal Mile, The Milkman's home at 52 Cockburn Street might look familiar as its striking curved frontage has appeared in films including *T2 Trainspotting*, *Fast & Furious 9* and *Avengers: Infinity War*.

Edinburgh-born artist Dear Prudence has immortalised the cafe's facade in a series of cards and postcards, which are painted using spent coffee grounds from the brew bar. They're available from the cafes' retail collections, which also include Bare Bones Chocolate, locally made ceramics and artisan soap.

ESTABLISHED
2020

KEY ROASTER
Origin Coffee Roasters

BREWING METHOD
Espresso, V60

MACHINE
La Marzocco Linea PB ABR

GRINDER
Mahlkonig EK43 S, Mythos One

OPENING HOURS
Mon–Fri
8am–5pm
Sat–Sun
9am–5pm

 Gluten FREE

 BEANS AVAILABLE INSTORE

 WIFI

 OUTDOOR SEATING

 DISABLED ACCESS

BRING YOUR OWN CUP

 DOG FRIENDLY

themilkman.coffee   **01314 661346**
f @themilkmancoffee   🐦 @themilkmanedin   @ @themilkmancoffee

70 UNION BREW LAB

6-8 South College Street, Edinburgh, EH8 9AA

This coffee shop and provisions store has been firmly pinned to Edinburgh's speciality coffee map for a decade.

Caffeine fans touring the capital have visited for a reliably decent coffee since it opened in 2012, and that loyalty only grew when Brew Lab partnered with Union Hand-Roasted Coffee in 2019.

In addition to the delights of its freshly roasted coffee, visitors and locals swing by to tuck into light lunches and explore the specialist coffee gear on display.

 LOW ON BEANS? FILL UP A CONTAINER AT THE COFFEE DISPENSARY

There are always two types of Union espresso up for grabs (one dialled in for milk, the other recommended for espresso or long blacks), plus a house batch brew. These are supported by a rotating roster of guest pourovers, which come via reputable roasteries such as Fortitude, Obadiah and Williams & Johnson.

Want to chase your coffee with something sweet? Check out the pastry and cake display stuffed with goods from local bakeries. Feast on the likes of spiced cinnamon buns from Nice Times Bakery, bejewelled brownies from 101 Bakery and plump vegan doughnuts crafted by Considerit.

ESTABLISHED
2012

KEY ROASTER
Union Hand-Roasted Coffee

BREWING METHOD
Espresso, batch brew, Kalita Wave

MACHINE
Victoria Arduino Black Eagle Gravitech

GRINDER
Mythos One, Mahlkonig EK43

OPENING HOURS
Mon-Sun
8am-6pm

 BEANS AVAILABLE

INSTORE

 WIFI

 DISABLED ACCESS

 BRING YOUR OWN Cup

 COFFEE COURSES

 DOG FRIENDLY

brewlabcoffee.co.uk   01316 628963

 @brewlabcoffee

71 LUCKIE BEANS

Haymarket Railway Station, Haymarket Terrace, Edinburgh, EH12 5EY

Commuters passing through Edinburgh's Haymarket Station grab their daily dose of quality caffeine from this indie cart which is known for its friendly baristas, creative latte art and award-winning brews.

The coffee is bronzed in a Giesen roaster at the Luckie Beans HQ in Galashiels. Make like a local and plump for the Love Lane house blend, a combination of beans from India, Kenya, Guatemala and Brazil. Single-origin fans should check out the Rwanda Dukunde Kawa Musasa, an award winner that delivers smooth and fruity notes of strawberry, passionfruit and guava.

 ASK FOR A DIRTY CHAI – AN AROMATIC CHAI BLEND SERVED WITH A SHOT OF ESPRESSO

While coffee is the main reason to make a pit stop at the cart (you can even grab bags of beans to take home), the crew also serve tea from Edinburgh-based Shibui, hot chocolate from The Real Hot Chocolate Company and vegan snacks from Raw Gorilla.

ESTABLISHED
2019

KEY ROASTER
Luckie Beans Coffee Roasters

BREWING METHOD
Espresso

MACHINE
La Marzocco Linea Classic

GRINDER
Mazzer Super Jolly

OPENING HOURS
Mon–Sat
6.30am–6.45pm
Sun
8am–2.30pm

 BEANS AVAILABLE INSTORE

 WIFI

 CYCLE FRIENDLY

 OUTDOOR SEATING

 DISABLED ACCESS

 DOG FRIENDLY

luckiebeans.co.uk   07810 446537

f @luckiebeans 🐦 @luckie_beans 📷 @luckie_beans

72 SALT CAFE

54-56 Morningside Road, Edinburgh, EH10 4BZ

This multi-award-winning Morningside cafe recently added another piece of silverware to its considerable collection when it scooped Best Cafe at the 2022 Edinburgh Evening News Restaurant Awards.

Salt's success is no surprise when you know that co-founder and head chef Steve Connolly-Bastock is a highly skilled butcher who has worked alongside leading chefs such as Aiden Byrne and Tom Kitchin.

Steve and wife Liv make almost everything served in their popular cafe from scratch – including sausages, dry-cured bacon, preserves, compotes and cakes.

 CHECK OUT NEW SISTER VENUE, PINCH OF SALT, LOCATED IN A CONVERTED POLICE BOX IN TOLLCROSS

This bounty is served as an all-day brunch menu (perfect for a weekend lie-in) that's split into sweet and savoury sections. Much-Instagrammed staples include the buttermilk pancakes and belly-busting butcher's breakfast.

Accompanying the first-rate food is speciality coffee roasted in the city by Mr Eion. The most indulgent way to sample the excellent house roast is in the luxe mocha, where it's paired with house-made dark truffle ganache.

ESTABLISHED
2020

KEY ROASTER
Mr Eion
Coffee Roaster

BREWING METHOD
Espresso,
batch brew,
cold brew

MACHINE
Rancilio Classe 7

GRINDER
Fiorenzato F64E

OPENING HOURS
Mon-Thu
8.30am-3pm
Fri
8.30am-4pm
Sat-Sun
9am-4pm

salt.scot 01316 295910
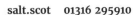 @salt.scot

EDINBURGH ROASTERIES
AND TRAINER
ROAS

73 CAIRNGORM COFFEE

27 Arthur Street, Edinburgh, EH6 5DA

The MO at this Edinburgh roastery – to ensure no one has to settle for average coffee – remains as relevant today as when the roastery opened in 2017.

To achieve this goal, Cairngorm founder Robi Lambie and co-owner Harris Grant continually build on their speciality coffee knowledge and use a roasting style that focuses on bringing out each lot's natural characteristics and flavour potential.

'A NEW COLOUR-CODED SYSTEM MAKES CHOOSING COFFEE SUPER SIMPLE'

Robi, Harris and the team have recently introduced a colour-coded system for their single origins, which makes choosing a coffee to suit your palate super simple. Red denotes syrupy red fruits, orange represents juicy citrus fruits, purple equals wild and funky, green means chocolatey and crowd-pleasing, and pink reveals the beans are a special release.

The team also cook up a range of blends, including the seasonal house espresso Guilty Pleasure. Its name references the idea that some baristas belittle blends but secretly love them. Whatever you order, read up on the beans' journey from farm to cup on the Cairngorm website.

ESTABLISHED
2017

ROASTER MAKE & SIZE
Probat 12kg

BEANS AVAILABLE
ONLINE

cairngorm.coffee
f @cairngormcoffee 🐦 @cairngormcoffee 📷 @cairngormcoffeeco

74 ARTISAN ROAST COFFEE ROASTERS

Unit 4 Peffermill Business Parc, 25 King's Haugh Road, Edinburgh, EH16 5UY

DIEDRICH

From humble beginnings roasting at its flagship Broughton Street store, Artisan has remained at the cutting edge of the Scottish speciality scene and is now one of the country's leading roasteries. The current set-up includes an enviable collection of drum-roasting machines overseen by a crack team who constantly hone their craft and skills – with knock-out results.

Working closely with Cup of Excellence head judge John Thompson, the gang source top-quality seasonal greens and strive for absolute consistency in every bag of freshly roasted beans. They implement a rigorous model of test-roasting and cupping to deliver diverse flavours and styles that represent the producers they work with.

'A CRACK TEAM WHO CONSTANTLY HONE THEIR CRAFT'

Welfare, social and environmental concerns have always been at the top of the Artisan agenda. Carefully forged long-term and sustainable relationships with coffee producers, innovative packaging solutions and a close partnership with Circular Coffee Scotland ensure Artisan Roast beans have a positive impact.

Taste the goods in person at Artisan's cafes in Leith, Stockbridge and Edinburgh's St James Quarter.

ESTABLISHED
2007

ROASTER MAKE & SIZE
Diedrich 12kg

Toper 30kg

Probat Probatino 1kg

Probat BRZ2 100g

Roest L100S

OPEN BY APPOINTMENT

COFFEE COURSES

BEANS AVAILABLE

ONLINE

artisanroast.co.uk   07514 167470

f @artisanroast   🐦 @artisanroast   📷 @artisanroastcoffeeroasters

CONTINUE YOUR ADVENTURES IN COFFEE

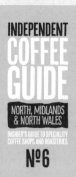

Discover the best speciality coffee shops and roasteries across the UK and Ireland with the Independent Coffee Guide series

INDYCOFFEE.GUIDE

75 COFFEE NEXUS

8 Howard Street, Edinburgh, EH3 5JP

For over a decade, Coffee Nexus has been *the* go-to for coffee training in the UK.

Under the expert guidance of its founder John Thompson, hundreds of coffee geeks have gained SCA-skills certification. Baristas, roasters and coffee businesses from across the UK make the trip to Edinburgh to extract knowledge from the Cup of Excellence head judge. John's extensive insight into the industry and frequent trips to origin equip him with the expertise to create solutions for speciality set-ups of all sizes.

ESTABLISHED
2009

COFFEE COURSES

COURSES

'REMOVING BARRIERS FOR SMALLER INDIE COFFEE BUSINESSES'

In-person courses at the SCA-certified premier training campus – designed for those looking to hone their green coffee, roasting and sensory skills – will recommence in 2023. There are also Q grading courses run by qualified CQI instructors.

With a handful of roasters and some serious analytical kit at their fingertips, the Coffee Nexus team also spend their time roasting, testing, measuring, grading and slurping. Removing barriers to testing and opening access to this type of service for smaller indie coffee businesses has always been important to the company and works hand-in-hand with Coffee Nexus' skill-building and training programmes.

coffeenexus.co.uk
f @coffeenexus 🐦 @coffeenexus 📷 @coffeenexus

23 EH9 ESPRESSO

MORE
GOOD
CUPS

So many exceptional places
to drink coffee ...

76 ARTISAN ROAST COFFEE ROASTERS – BROUGHTON STREET

57 Broughton Street, Edinburgh, EH1 3RJ
artisanroast.co.uk

77 ARTISAN ROAST COFFEE ROASTERS – BRUNTSFIELD PLACE

138 Bruntsfield Place,
Edinburgh, EH10 4ER
artisanroast.co.uk

78 ARTISAN ROAST COFFEE ROASTERS – LEITH WALK

72–74 Leith Walk, Edinburgh, EH6 5HB
artisanroast.co.uk

79 ARTISAN ROAST COFFEE ROASTERS – STOCKBRIDGE

100a Raeburn Place, Edinburgh, EH4 1HH
artisanroast.co.uk

80 BLACK PINE COFFEE CO.

518 Great Western Road,
Glasgow, G12 8EL
blackpine.coffee

81 BONNIE & WILD

St James Quarter (level 4), 415–417
St James Crescent, Edinburgh, EH1 3AE
bonnieandwildmarket.com

82 BRAMBLERS

21 Salamander Place, Edinburgh, EH6 7JJ
bramblers.scot

83 BREW PAISLEY

3 County Place, Paisley,
Renfrewshire, PA1 1BN
brewpaisley.co.uk

84 BROKEN CLOCK CAFE & PATISSERIE

10 Park Road, Glasgow, G4 9JG
brokenclockcafe.co.uk

85 CAIRNGORM COFFEE – MELVILLE PLACE

1 Melville Place, Edinburgh, EH3 7PR
cairngorm.coffee

86 CASTELLO COFFEE CO.

7–8 Barclay Terrace,
Edinburgh, EH10 4HP

87 CULT ESPRESSO

104 Buccleuch Street,
Edinburgh, EH8 9NQ
cult-espresso.com

88 FORTITUDE COFFEE – HAMILTON PLACE

66 Hamilton Place, Stockbridge,
Edinburgh, EH3 5AZ
fortitudecoffee.com

89 FORTITUDE COFFEE – YORK PLACE

3c York Place, Edinburgh, EH1 3EB
fortitudecoffee.com

90 GRAIN AND GRIND – CATHCART

109 Clarkston Road, Glasgow, G44 3BL
grainandgrind.co.uk

91 GRAIN AND GRIND – INVERNESS

1 Tomnahurich Street,
Inverness, IV3 5DA
grainandgrind.co.uk

92 GRAIN AND GRIND – STRATHBUNGO

742 Pollokshaws Road,
Glasgow, G41 2AD
grainandgrind.co.uk

93 GRANARY CAFE – LINLITHGOW

102 High Street, Linlithgow,
West Lothian, EH49 7AQ

94 KEMBER & JONES

134 Byres Road, Glasgow, G12 8TD
shop.kemberandjones.co.uk

95 LABORATORIO ESPRESSO

93 West Nile Street, Glasgow, G1 2SH
laboratorioespresso.com

96 LOVECRUMBS

155 West Port, Edinburgh, EH3 9DP
lovecrumbs.co.uk

97 MACHINA

38 Marchmont Road,
Edinburgh, EH9 1HX
machina-coffee.com

98 MAYZE – FINNIESTON

974 Argyle Street, Finnieston,
Glasgow, G3 8LU
mayze.co.uk

99 PAPERCUP COFFEE COMPANY

603 Great Western Road,
Glasgow, G12 8HX
papercupcoffee.co.uk

100 PILGRIMS COFFEE

Marygate, Holy Island,
Northumberland, TD15 2SJ
pilgrimscoffee.com

101 SHORT LONG BLACK

501 Victoria Road, Glasgow, G42 8RL

102 SPACE SPECIALITY COFFEE HOUSE

540 Dumbarton Road, Glasgow, G11 6SW

103 SPRIGG - INGRAM STREET

241 Ingram Street, Glasgow, G1 1DA
sprigg.co.uk

104 TÀRMACHAN CAFE

Quarry Studios, Crathie,
Aberdeenshire, AB35 5UL
tarmachancafe.com

105 THE BEARDED BAKER

46 Rodney Street, Edinburgh, EH7 4DX
thebeardedbaker.co.uk

106 THE MAINSTREET TRADING COMPANY

Mainstreet Trading, St Boswells,
Melrose, Scottish Borders, TD6 OAT
mainstreetbooks.co.uk

107 THE SOURCE COFFEE CO.

4 Spittal Street, Edinburgh, EH3 9DX
thesourcecoffee.co.uk

108 TORO COFFEE

1484 Pollokshaws Road,
Glasgow, G43 1RE

109 UNORTHODOX ROASTERS – KINROSS

129 High Street, Kinross, KY13 8AQ
unorthodoxroasters.co.uk

110 UNORTHODOX ROASTERS – STIRLING

12 Friars Street, Stirling, FK8 1HA
unorthodoxroasters.co.uk

111 WE ARE ZEST

95 South Street, St Andrews,
Fife, EY16 9QW
wearezest.co.uk

112 WILLIAMS & JOHNSON COFFEE CO.

1 Customs Wharf, Edinburgh, EH6 6AL
williamsandjohnson.com

MORE GOOD ROASTERIES

Additional places to source beans
for your home hopper ...

113 COMMON COFFEE

Unit 7, Rosemains Steading, Pathhead,
Midlothian, EH37 5UQ
commoncoffee.co.uk

114 FAODAIL ROASTERY

Glasgow
faodailroastery.co.uk

115 FIGMENT

70 Countesswells Road,
Aberdeen, AB15 7YJ
figmentcoffee.com

116 GLEN LYON COFFEE ROASTERS

Aberfeldy Business Park, Dunkeld Road,
Aberfeldy, Perthshire, PH15 2AQ
glenlyoncoffee.co.uk

117 GRAIN AND GRIND

1 Tomnahurich Street, Inverness, IV3 5DA
grainandgrind.co.uk

118 MACHINA COFFEE ROASTERS

Unit 9 Peffermill Parc, 25 King's Haugh,
Edinburgh, EH16 5UY
machina-coffee.com

119 OBADIAH COFFEE

Unit 4-5 The Arches, Abbeyhill,
Edinburgh, EH8 8EE
obadiahcoffee.com

120 PAPERCUP COFFEE ROASTERS

Unit 8, Archway 17, 100 Eastvale Place,
SWG3, Glasgow, G3 8QG
papercupcoffee.co.uk

121 PILGRIMS COFFEE

Marygate, Holy Island,
Northumberland, TD15 2SJ
pilgrimscoffee.com

122 SPEYSIDE COFFEE ROASTING CO.

Kirk Cottage, South Road, Garmouth,
Moray, IV32 7LU
speysidecoffee.co.uk

123 STEAMPUNK COFFEE ROASTERS

49a Kirk Ports, North Berwick,
East Lothian, EH39 4HL
steampunkcoffee.co.uk

124 THE GATEHOUSE COFFEE ROASTERS

Benn Avenue, Paisley,
Renfrewshire, PA1 1JS
thegatehousecoffeeroasters.com

125 THE GOOD COFFEE CARTEL

12 Cornwall Street, Glasgow, G41 1AQ
thegoodcoffeecartel.com

126 THE SOURCE COFFEE CO.

4 Spittal Street, Edinburgh, EH3 9DX
thesourcecoffee.co.uk

127 UNORTHODOX ROASTERS

129 High Street, Kinross, KY13 8AQ
unorthodoxroasters.co.uk

128 WILLIAMS & JOHNSON COFFEE CO.

1 Customs Wharf, Edinburgh, EH6 6AL
williamsandjohnson.com

MEET OUR COMMITTEE

The *Independent Coffee Guide Scotland*'s committee is made up of a small band of leading coffee experts and the team at Salt Media, who have worked with the Scottish coffee community to produce this guide.

LISA LAWSON

JOHN THOMPSON

JAMES AITKEN

Dear Green Coffee Roasters founder Lisa has been at the forefront of the Scottish speciality scene since she began roasting in Glasgow in 2011.

Through many extra-curricular projects, such as launching Glasgow Coffee Festival, UK Coffee Roasting Championship and Scottish AeroPress Championships (as well as helping establish the first *Independent Coffee Guide Scotland*), Lisa's been one of the catalysts for the city's vibrant coffee culture.

In addition to running her Glasgow roastery, in 2021 the authorised SCA trainer continued her environmental campaign by overseeing Dear Green being certified as a B Corp.

John works with coffee roasters, brands and farmers to improve sustainability, manage ongoing quality and add value to coffee.

He's head judge for the Cup of Excellence programme, and his Edinburgh training lab Coffee Nexus was the first in Scotland to be certified as an SCA premier training campus for sensory, green coffee and roasting.

John has written educational content for the SCA for 11 years, as well as offering its training courses at his Edinburgh HQ.

Coffee Nexus also helps smaller roasteries access a range of often out-of-reach analytical tools and supports them with product development and consultancy.

James started his coffee career in 2004 at Matthew Algie where he specialised in machine repair, installations and barista training.

After ten years of machine mechanics, he took a break from servicing to join the roasting team at Dear Green in Glasgow.

In 2017, James launched Us V Them through which he installs, sells and repairs coffee machines across Scotland.

In 2020 he opened an Us V Them HQ in Glasgow, which includes a slick espresso bar, workshop and showroom. A sister cafe opened within McLellan Galleries on Sauchiehall Street in 2022.

James is also a certified AST for the SCA Coffee Technicians Program.

INDEX

Entry no

U-Z

FOR BREW FREAKS, BEAN GEEKS

AND THE SIMPLY CURIOUS ...